ORGANIZING FOR LEARNING

CLASSROOM TECHNIQUES TO HELP STUDENTS INTERACT WITHIN SMALL GROUPS

ORGANIZING FOR LEARNING

CLASSROOM TECHNIQUES TO HELP STUDENTS INTERACT WITHIN SMALL GROUPS

Deana Senn
Robert J. Marzano

With Libby H. Garst and Carla Moore

LearningSciences
MARZANO
CENTER

1400 Centrepark Blvd, Suite 1000
West Palm Beach, FL 33401
717-845-6300

email: pub@learningsciences.com
learningsciences.com

Printed in the United States of America

20 19 18 17 16 15   2 3 4

Publisher's Cataloging-in-Publication Data

Senn, Deana.
  Organizing for learning : classroom techniques to help students interact within small groups / Deana Senn [and] Robert J. Marzano.
    pages cm
  ISBN: 978-1-941112-02-1 (pbk.)
1. Group work in education—United States. 2. Team learning approach in education. 3. Effective teaching. 4. Education—Study and teaching. 5. Classroom management.   I. Marzano, Robert J. II. Title.
  LB1032 .S435 2015
  371.395—dc23
                              [2015932267]

MARZANO CENTER

Essentials for Achieving Rigor SERIES

The *Essentials for Achieving Rigor* series of instructional guides helps educators become highly skilled at implementing, monitoring, and adapting instruction. Put it to practical use immediately, adopting day-to-day examples as models for application in your own classroom.

Books in the series:

Identifying Critical Content: Classroom Techniques to Help Students Know What Is Important

Examining Reasoning: Classroom Techniques to Help Students Produce and Defend Claims

Recording & Representing Knowledge: Classroom Techniques to Help Students Accurately Organize and Summarize Content

Examining Similarities & Differences: Classroom Techniques to Help Students Deepen Their Understanding

Processing New Information: Classroom Techniques to Help Students Engage With Content

Revising Knowledge: Classroom Techniques to Help Students Examine Their Deeper Understanding

Practicing Skills, Strategies & Processes: Classroom Techniques to Help Students Develop Proficiency

Engaging in Cognitively Complex Tasks: Classroom Techniques to Help Students Generate & Test Hypotheses Across Disciplines

Creating & Using Learning Targets & Performance Scales: How Teachers Make Better Instructional Decisions

Organizing for Learning: Classroom Techniques to Help Students Interact Within Small Groups

Dedication

I dedicate this book to my nieces, Tara and Lyla. I am so lucky to have the most dedicated, brilliant, athletic, and prettiest nieces on earth. I love you both (equally)!

—Deana Senn

Table of Contents

Acknowledgments

Learning Sciences International would like to thank the following reviewers:

Anne E. Hasse
2014 Wisconsin Elementary Teacher
   of the Year
Wakanda Elementary School
Menomonie, Wisconsin

Kristen Karszes
2013 Beaufort County Teacher of the
   Year
Hilton Head Island High School
Beaufort, South Carolina

Diana Leddy
2009 Vermont Teacher of the Year
The Newton School
South Strafford, Vermont

Beth Maloney
2014 Arizona Teacher of the Year
Sunset Hills Elementary School
Surprise, Arizona

Daniele Massey
2013 Teacher of the Year
Department of Defense Education
   Activity

Heidi Welch
2013 New Hampshire Teacher of the
   Year
Hillsboro-Deering High School
Hillsboro, New Hampshire

About the Authors

DEANA SENN, MSSE, is an expert in instructional strategies and classroom assessments. She is the Instructional Designer and Staff Developer for Learning Sciences International. Ms. Senn's curriculum, instruction, and assessment experience spans the United States and Canada. Ms. Senn has been a teacher and leader in school, district, regional, and provincial roles in both rural and urban settings. She is a graduate of Texas A&M University and received her master's degree from Montana State University. With her extensive experience focusing on teaching and learning, Ms. Senn offers a unique perspective for improving instructional practice.

ROBERT J. MARZANO, PhD, is CEO of Marzano Research Laboratory and Executive Director of the Learning Sciences Marzano Center for Teacher and Leader Evaluation. A leading researcher in education, he is a speaker, trainer, and author of more than 150 articles on topics such as instruction, assessment, writing and implementing standards, cognition, effective leadership, and school intervention. He has authored over 30 books, including *The Art and Science of Teaching* (ASCD, 2007) and *Teacher Evaluation That Makes a Difference* (ASCD, 2013).

LIBBY H. GARST, MSEd, creates professional development for teacher growth as a Staff Developer and Instructional Designer for Learning Sciences Marzano Center. She has been a successful teacher and instructional coach. She graduated from Virginia Tech and received her master's degree at the University of Virginia.

CARLA MOORE, MSEd, oversees content and product development for Learning Sciences International, with a special emphasis on teacher and administrator effectiveness. She received her bachelor's degree from Valdosta State College.

Introduction

This guide, *Organizing for Learning: Classroom Techniques to Help Students Interact Within Small Groups*, is intended as a resource for improving a specific strategy of instructional practice: organizing for learning.

Your motivation to incorporate this strategy into your instructional toolbox may have come from a personal desire to improve your instructional practice through the implementation of a research-based set of strategies (such as those found in the Marzano instructional framework) or a desire to increase the rigor of the instructional strategies you implement in your class so that students meet the expectations of demanding standards such as the Common Core State Standards, Next Generation Science Standards, C3 Framework for Social Studies State Standards, or state standards based on or influenced by College and Career Readiness Anchor Standards.

This guide will help teachers of all grade levels and subjects improve their performance of a specific instructional strategy: organizing for learning. Narrowing your focus on a specific skill, such as organizing for learning, will enable you to concentrate on the nuances of this instructional strategy to deliberately improve it. This allows you to intentionally plan, implement, monitor, adapt, and reflect on this single element of your instructional practice. A person seeking to become an expert displays distinctive behaviors, as explained by Marzano and Toth (2013):

- breaks down the specific skills required to be an expert

- focuses on improving those particular critical skill chunks (as opposed to easy tasks) during practice or day-to-day activities

- receives immediate, specific, and actionable feedback, particularly from a more experienced coach

- continually practices each critical skill at more challenging levels with the intention of mastering it, giving far less time to skills already mastered

This series of guides will support each of the previously listed behaviors, with a focus on breaking down the specific skills required to be an expert and giving day-to-day practical suggestions to enhance these skills.

Building on the Marzano Instructional Model

This series is based on the Marzano instructional framework, which is grounded in research and provides educators with the tools they need to connect instructional practice to student achievement. The series uses key terms that are specific to the Marzano model of instruction. See Table 1, Glossary of Key Terms.

Table 1: Glossary of Key Terms

Term	Definition
CCSS	Common Core State Standards is the official name of the standards documents developed by the Common Core State Standards Initiative (CCSSI), the goal of which is to prepare students in the United States for college and career.
CCR	College and Career Readiness Anchor Standards are broad statements that incorporate individual standards for various grade levels and specific areas.
Desired result	The intended result for the student(s) due to the implementation of a specific strategy.
Monitoring	The act of checking for evidence of the desired result of a specific strategy while the strategy is being implemented.
Instructional strategy	A category of techniques used for classroom instruction that has been proven to have a high probability of enhancing student achievement.
Instructional technique	The method used to teach and deepen understanding of knowledge and skills.
Content	The knowledge and skills necessary for students to demonstrate standards.
Scaffolding	A purposeful progression of support that targets cognitive complexity and student autonomy to reach rigor.
Extending	Activities that move students who have already demonstrated the desired result to a higher level of understanding.

The educational pendulum swings widely from decade to decade. Educators move back and forth between prescriptive checklists and step-by-step lesson plans to approaches that encourage instructional autonomy with minimal regard for the science of teaching and the need for accountability. Two practices are often missing in both of these approaches to defining effective instruction: 1) specific statements of desired results and 2) solid research-based connections. The Marzano instructional framework provides a comprehensive system that details what is required from teachers to develop their craft using research-based instructional strategies. Launching from this solid instructional foundation, teachers will then be prepared to merge that science with their own unique, yet effective, instructional style, which is the art of teaching.

Organizing for Learning: Classroom Techniques to Help Students Interact Within Small Groups will help you grow into an innovative and highly skilled teacher who is able to implement, scaffold, and extend instruction to meet a range of student needs.

Essentials for Achieving Rigor

This series of guides details essential classroom strategies to support the complex shifts in teaching that are necessary for an environment where academic rigor is a requirement for all students. The instructional strategies presented in this series are essential to effectively teach the CCSS, the Next Generation Science Standards, or standards designated by your school district or state. They require a deeper understanding, more effective use of strategies, and greater frequency of implementation for your students to demonstrate the knowledge and skills required by rigorous standards. This series includes instructional techniques appropriate for all grade levels and content areas. The examples contained within are grade-level specific and should serve as models and launching points for application in your own classroom.

Your skillful implementation of these strategies is essential to your students' mastery of the CCSS or other rigorous standards, no matter the grade level or subject you are teaching. Other instructional strategies covered in the Essentials for Achieving Rigor series, such as examining reasoning and engaging students in cognitively complex tasks, exemplify the cognitive complexity needed to meet rigorous standards. Taken as a package, these strategies may at first glance seem quite daunting. For this reason, the series focuses on just one strategy in each guide.

Organizing for Learning

Organizing for learning is a powerful instructional strategy that focuses on facilitating small-group discussions in which students use academic language to talk about content with each other. This strategy can be a formal organization of students as well as informal conversations in small groups and with partners. This strategy does *not* encompass whole-class discussions, even if students talk to each other during them. While there is a time and place during instruction for teachers to lead whole-class dialogue, this strategy is focused on smaller groups of students interacting with each other rather than the teacher.

When asking students to interact with each other, consider the type of knowledge you want them to learn as they work together. Declarative knowledge consists of facts that students need to understand. If you want students to work with partners or small groups to interact with declarative knowledge during their group work, they can readily discuss information and share ideas at any point during your lesson. However, if you want students to interact with each other to learn procedural knowledge, they will need to first work individually. After they have had opportunities to process their own thinking, they can then meet with their peer(s) to check for accuracy and discuss their own perspectives.

There must be a stated purpose for interaction when you organize students to work together. The purpose might be for students to process new content, practice a procedure, or even revise their thinking. Therefore, organizing for learning almost always goes hand in hand with other instructional strategies such as helping students process content; helping students practice skills, strategies, and processes; or helping students revise knowledge. When two or more instructional strategies are used simultaneously in a lesson, the combination is known as a *macrostrategy*. However, no matter which strategy you pair with organizing for learning, you must first determine how you want students to interact. Students can interact in two ways: collaboratively and cooperatively.

Collaborative Learning

Collaborative learning is interaction in which students share ideas and consider other perspectives as they are learning. In this type of learning, there is low task interdependence. Students may be asked to share or reminded to stay on task, but their success in completing a task is not immediately tied to their productivity during collaboration. At times, having little or no task accountability is necessary for students to be comfortable with risk taking. Be clear, however, that there are still expectations for participating and learning. The absence of a completed work product does not mean that students can opt out of participating. Put structures in place to ensure that all students participate and that groups remain focused.

Cooperative Learning

Cooperative learning is interaction designed to facilitate the accomplishment of a specific end product or goal through students working together. This type of grouping has higher accountability levels since there is usually a task or a product that the group is expected to produce. This type of group work is also called *productive group work*. Productive group work can have group and/or individual accountability and is useful when you want students to consolidate their thinking and understanding. When students are expected to complete a work product, plan more extensive periods for interaction in which they can grapple with their thinking and apply what they are learning. Knowing the difference between cooperative and collaborative learning will help you understand how the purpose of each technique determines the manner in which students will interact with one another.

Some students may not have had opportunities in previous grades to work with their peers as an integral part of the learning process. They may have only been asked to work independently or with teacher assistance and not been required or encouraged to share their ideas with peers. Because of this, many students will lack the skills necessary for effective group work. Generally, the skills individuals use to combine what they know with how they feel to better function in society are known as *conative skills*. These skills are also necessary for group work and should be taught and supported as part of the routines you teach students for how to interact with each other during learning. Table 2 displays a list of conative skills, and they are discussed in more detail as they apply to each of the techniques in this guide.

Table 2: Conative Skills

Becoming aware of the power of interpretation
Cultivating a growth mindset
Cultivating resiliency
Avoiding negative thinking
Taking various perspectives
Interacting responsibly
Handling controversy and conflict resolution

Marzano, Carbaugh, Rutherford & Toth, 2014.

The Effective Implementation of Organizing for Learning

Positive interdependence results when students recognize that their success is linked to the success of the members of their group and is an essential prerequisite for effective student interaction (Johnson, 1975). When students perceive that every group member is indispensable to achieving their mutual goals and that they are both dependent on and obliged to their peers, conditions are ripe for collaborative learning (Frey, Fisher, & Everlove, 2009). Creating conditions and setting the stage for positive interdependence as students work with peers is a high priority as you organize your students for learning.

Give students a specific purpose each time they interact. Students' understanding of the purpose for their grouping will facilitate the positive interdependence necessary for effective students' interactions. Consider the details of when, where, why, and how you want students to interact with each other in advance of the interaction. The techniques in this guide are designed to facilitate this. As you read through the techniques, notice that their order reflects their intentionality for increasing cognitive complexity. When students focus on declarative knowledge by being asked to recall or comprehend, techniques that focus on collaborative discussions will work best. As learning progresses, you should ask students to interact for longer periods of time and in more extensive ways using more cooperative techniques. The ordering of techniques reflects this, with the techniques ultimately leading to students interacting as they focus on metacognition.

The following teacher behaviors are essential to the effective implementation of organizing for learning:

- identifying critical content

- planning meaningful tasks

- structuring intentional interactions

- organizing students into groups

- establishing routines

- teaching and reinforcing conative skills

As you prepare to effectively implement this strategy, think first about how to avoid the following common mistakes. These roadblocks can take your teaching, and ultimately your students' learning, off course.

- The teacher fails to identify the critical content.

- The teacher fails to structure purposeful student interaction.

- The teacher fails to prepare students to interact in groups.

- The teacher fails to stay out of the conversation.

Failing to Identify Critical Content

As you plan to group students, you can easily overlook mentally walking through the entire process beforehand. You might think about what you want groups of students to work on or how you want them to interact. However, for interaction to be purposeful, you must intentionally select the critical content you want students to learn, deepen, or use.

Failing to Structure Purposeful Student Interaction

Teachers may think that students will structure themselves to work collaboratively or cooperatively, but that is often not the case. Students need structure and guidance for how to purposefully interact with each other. To structure purposeful student interaction, specify what task students will work on in their groups, and then identify how you will structure students' interactions with each other.

Failing to Prepare Students to Interact in Groups

You may assume that because your students are skilled at interacting in social situations, they will also know how to interact during academic situations. However, students can often be shy about their knowledge or not know how to express themselves in respectful ways when disagreements occur. Prepare students to interact in groups by teaching the routines specific to group work as well as the applicable conative skills they need to be prepared for the emotional aspects of collaborating and interacting with their peers.

Failing to Stay out of the Conversation

Taking charge of a group as you approach it is a mistake. The result is quite often a conversation between you and a single member of the group. Or, you may take charge of the entire group and begin talking, simply expecting the students to listen. If you are the person talking, you will miss opportunities to determine whether your students have the knowledge and skills you have been teaching. Although you may well have rich conversations with students in small groups, the purpose of the interactions is for students to have these conversations with each other. If you are not in the habit of taking a back seat as you go from group to group, you will find that your students get quiet when you approach their group because they are used to you taking charge. Instead, simply ask them to continue their conversation. If students are unaccustomed to your listening in on their conversations, they may initially be reluctant. However, with a few guiding questions and a reminder to answer to their group, not you, they will soon begin to talk freely in front of you.

Monitoring for the Desired Result

As an essential part of implementation, do more than merely organize students into small groups. During their interactions, you must intentionally monitor to make sure students are enhancing their understanding of the critical content as a result of their interactions. Please do not multitask during the all-important opportunities you have to determine whether students understand what you are teaching them. Walk around and listen. Focus on the academic language your students use to determine whether they understand the critical content and are able to make connections between concepts. Note any misconceptions that may be widespread among students and be sure to correct them immediately. There are several ways teachers can monitor whether students are interacting effectively to enhance their understanding of critical content:

- Students use academic language to talk about content with each other.

- Students share perspectives about critical content.

- Students know their responsibilities during group work.

- Students share the workload equally.

- Students use small-group interaction to enhance their learning.

Scaffolding and Extending Instruction to Meet Students' Needs

As you monitor for the desired result of each technique, you will likely realize that some students are not as effective in their interactions as they need to be. Others are easily able to demonstrate the desired result of specific techniques. Equipped with this knowledge, adapt the various techniques to meet the needs of students for whom scaffolds or extensions are necessary.

There are four different categories of support you can provide for students who need scaffolding: 1) support that teachers (including instructional aides or other paraprofessionals) or peers provide; 2) support that teachers provide by manipulating the difficulty level of content or interactions (e.g., providing an easier reading level that contains the same content); 3) breaking down the content or interaction into smaller chunks to make it more manageable; and 4) giving students organizers to clarify and guide their thinking through a task one step at a time (Dickson, Collins, Simmons & Kame'enui, 1998).

Within each technique described in this guide, there are examples of ways to scaffold and extend instruction to meet the needs of your students. *Scaffolding* provides support that targets cognitive complexity, student autonomy, and rigor. *Extending* moves students who have already demonstrated the desired result to a higher level of interaction and understanding. These examples are provided as suggestions, and you should adapt them to target the specific needs of your students. Use them to spark ideas as you plan to meet the needs of your English language learners, students who receive special education or lack home support, or simply the student who was absent the day before. The extension activities can help you plan for students in your gifted and talented program or those with a keen interest in the subject matter you are teaching.

Teacher Self-Reflection

As you develop expertise in organizing students to learn, reflecting on your skill level and effectiveness can help you become more successful in implementing this strategy. Use the following set of reflection questions to guide you. The questions begin simply, with reflecting on how to start the implementation process, and move to progressively more complex ways of organizing students to learn.

1. How can you begin to incorporate some aspect of this strategy in your instruction?

2. How can you structure purposeful student interaction about critical content?

3. How can you monitor the extent to which students share perspectives about critical content?

4. What are some ways you can adapt organizing students to learn that address unique student needs and situations?

5. What are you learning about your students as you organize them to learn?

Instructional Techniques to Organize Students to Learn

There are many options for how to organize students to learn with the ultimate goal being their mastery of the learning targets of your grade level or content. The approaches you choose to use during a specific lesson or unit will depend on the grade you teach, content involved, and makeup of your class. These various approaches are called *instructional techniques.* This guide provides the logistics, routines, and support you need as you implement the following techniques:

- Instructional Technique 1: Partner Discussions

- Instructional Technique 2: Grouping for Active Processing

- Instructional Technique 3: Paired Practice

- Instructional Technique 4: Structured Grouping

- Instructional Technique 5: Cooperative Projects

- Instructional Technique 6: Peer Response Groups

- Instructional Technique 7: Group Reflecting on Learning

All of the techniques are similarly organized and include the following components:

- a brief introduction to the technique

- ways to effectively implement the technique

- common mistakes to avoid as you implement the technique

- examples and nonexamples from elementary and secondary classrooms using selected learning targets or standards from various documents

- ways to monitor for the desired result

- a scale for monitoring students

- ways to scaffold and extend instruction to meet the needs of students

Instructional Technique 1

PARTNER DISCUSSIONS

Partner discussion is often one of the first techniques that teachers use to facilitate peer-to-peer interaction. It requires little prep time and can be an excellent entry point to having your students interact with each other during learning. In this technique, there is limited group accountability. Students may be asked to share their perspectives with the class after their partner interactions, but they are not usually asked to turn in a work product as a result of their interactions.

Sharing perspectives with peers is a key aspect of learning new content. Asking students to respond to prompts and then share information with peers allows them to experience multiple perspectives. Sharing with partners allows students to see how others interact with and process information, enlarging and even changing their own understandings. Shared experiences, such as partner discussions, are essential building blocks of the teaching–learning process (Marzano & Brown, 2009).

How to Effectively Implement Partner Discussions

Recall the six teacher behaviors needed for the essential implementation of organizing for learning that were listed in the introduction. They are noted here to refresh your memory: 1) identifying critical content, 2) planning meaningful tasks, 3) structuring intentional interactions, 4) organizing students into groups, 5) establishing routines for interacting, and 6) teaching and reinforcing conative skills. The following sections describe each of these behaviors as they apply specifically to implementing partner discussions.

Identify Critical Content
Determining the specific aspect of critical content that you want students to discuss is the first step in the implementation of partner discussions. Use the learning target you have selected to help you identify that content. Student interactions must have a specific purpose and that purpose should be linked

to the learning target. If you are vague about what content you want students to discuss with their partners, your students will be confused regarding the point of their interactions.

Plan a Meaningful Task

Answering questions the teacher poses is one of the most common ways to facilitate partner discussions. To maximize the quantity and quality of your students' interaction, develop questions that require more than a single-word response. Single-word responses foster choppy interactions that interfere with the flow or give and take during conversation. One way to introduce quality questions is to periodically embed an open-ended response question during direct instruction. Frame questions that are cognitively complex and require extended responses. Open-ended response questions have two advantages: 1) they give your students opportunities to be active learners and 2) you are able to listen in as students talk to each other, immediately knowing whether students are learning what you want them to gain from the lesson. Rich conversations result when students discuss their complex thinking. If students do not have previous experiences interacting with one another as they learn and process content, they may be nervous about sharing ideas with their peers. Teach your students how to engage in productive conversations by modeling how to carry on rich conversations.

Structure Intentional Interactions

After you have identified the critical content and determined the question or prompt that will spark a conversation about the critical content, decide how you will structure student interaction during partner discussions. Structure which partner talks first and how long each partner talks. Instruct students in how to take turns talking and responding to their partners' statements. Routines are essential during intentional interaction to prevent individual students from grabbing the spotlight from their partners.

If you want to rearrange partners periodically without moving desks, seat students in groups of four, and then direct them to talk to either their side or across partners. Figure 1.1 illustrates a desk arrangement for designating side and across partners.

Figure 1.1: Sample Desk Arrangement for Designating Partners

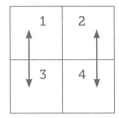

A variation of partner discussion is Think-Pair-Share (Kagan, 2009) in which students think about their response to a prompt before they pair with another student to share their thinking. The teacher asks students to share their thinking with the class. A second variation of partner discussion is Read-Write-Pair-Share in which students read, write a response, engage in partner conversation, and then share their ideas with the whole class. This type of partner sharing allows students to record or represent their thinking before sharing it with others, giving them additional time for individual processing. If you use this variation, allow adequate time for students to read and formulate their responses.

A less formal variation of partner discussion is a simple Turn and Talk. Students turn to someone near them and answer the question or prompt you posed. Turn and Talk is not structured as to who goes first or how long each partner will talk. Many times this form of partner interaction comes about once routines are in place and students are used to engaging in academic conversations with each other. If your students are new to interacting with each other, use one of the more formal variations of this technique. If your students have mastered the logistics of partner discussions, you can relax some of the routines and try variations.

Organize Students Into Groups

Think ahead about how you plan to partner students. A common approach is to partner students heterogeneously, assigning academically stronger students to work with students who may be struggling. Use assessment data from a unit pretest or results from previous units to help you make your decisions. Use more than just the total number of right or wrong answers as you analyze data. Focus on which concepts students have mastered and which ones still need more instruction or practice. Students who struggle with different types of foundational knowledge might comprise a good pair because they can lift each other up. Partnering two students who struggle with the same concepts might help you target your time when you help students. Place two students with exceptional backgrounds together to give them both incentives to excel. Be intentional as you make decisions based on the data you use.

Establish Routines

Classroom routines are often second nature to experienced teachers, and if you fall into that category, you may have forgotten how much time and effort you spent initially thinking about and establishing routines in your class-room. If you are new to asking your student to interact with each other as part of the learning process, think about which rules and procedures specific to partner interaction that you want to establish. The routines you presently use, such as raise your hand to be called on and do not talk to each to each other, are not applicable in this technique. Carefully select the rules and procedures you want to establish with students such as how to wait your turn, when to listen respectfully, and the necessity of keeping conversations focused on critical content. Teach and model those routines until students understand precisely when and how they apply.

In classrooms where collaboration and cooperation are the norm, students will usually go into and out of partner discussions several times during a lesson. Therefore, arrange your seating chart and desk configurations so that students can easily work with the partners you have selected for them. Thinking ahead about how students will be grouped and desks will be arranged can save precious instructional time. Establish routines around group work; for example, which direction the seats face, which partner moves, and what students should do if their partner is absent. The time you spend establishing these routines from the onset will help ensure that students interact responsibly and productively from the beginning and help to create a culture of collaboration and cooperation in your classroom.

Teach and Reinforce Conative Skills

Take time early in the year to teach students good listening skills to include the skill of active listening. Listening skills are behaviors such as looking at the person talking, not interrupting, and not getting distracted. Elementary teachers often teach these skills in the early primary grades, but teachers at upper grade levels sometimes forget to reinforce them. While the language used to describe and teach listening skills might change as students mature, the desired behaviors for good listening remain the same.

In addition to the common listening skills previously mentioned, teach and model for students how to take listening one step further to become active listeners. Active listening involves not only hearing and understanding what the speaker says, but also helping the speaker articulate thoughts and find solutions to the stated problems. Demonstrate active listening to your class by modeling the roles in three steps:

1. The speaker answers the prompt.

2. The active listener restates the answer in her own words.

3. The active listener elaborates on the original answer.

Once students have observed active listening modeled for them, provide positive feedback when you see this behavior in action.

Common Mistakes

There are several common mistakes teachers can make when facilitating partner discussions:

- The teacher does not provide a specific question for students to answer.

- The teacher asks questions that do not require discussion.

- The teacher gives students answers to the questions instead of listening to their answers.

- The teacher allows students to lose their focus on the critical content of the lesson.

- The teacher does not teach, model, and regularly use routines for which partner talks first or how long each partner should talk.

- The teacher calls on every student to share after the discussion.

Examples and Nonexamples of Grouping for Partner Discussions

Following are two sets of examples and nonexamples (one elementary and one secondary) of how you can use the partner discussion technique in classrooms. As you are reading the examples, keep in mind the common mistakes that you can make while implementing this strategy, and also consider how an example teacher might monitor for the desired results.

Elementary Example of Partner Discussions

This example features a first-grade teacher facilitating a partner discussion related to the following learning target: *using observations, explain how young plants and animals are similar but not the same as their parents.* This learning target aligns with the standard: *Make observations to construct an evidence-based account that young plants and animals are like, but not exactly like, their parents* (NGSS 1-LS3-1).

The teacher uses partner discussion often in his classroom, so students are comfortable with the routine of talking to their peers. The desks are arranged in groups of four so that students have quick access to two different partners. He prepares for the lesson by printing class sets of two photos. One photo is of a young and mature oak tree and the other is of a man and his baby boy. He ensures that each set of partners has the two photographs at their desks. He has also made sure that each set of partners has blue and red crayons or pencils.

> Class, today we are going to observe how young babies and plants are like, but not the same as, their parents. To do this, I want you to all look at the picture of the baby and the father. Think about how they are the same. Think about things they both have. For instance they both have two hands. Now, you can't use that example, because I did. But, what else do they both have? Think about it. It's not time to share with your partner yet.

After giving students a moment to compose their responses, the teacher continues his directions.

When I give the signal, turn to the person beside you, your side partner, and explain what you saw in the picture that is the same for the baby and the father. When your partner is talking, listen with your entire body like we've practiced. After you both speak, agree on what is similar about the baby and the man and circle those parts of the picture with blue. Remember that you both can't talk at the same time. On my signal, I want the person closest to the front of the room to speak first. When you are done, please let your partner explain what he or she sees that is the same between the pictures.

The teacher rings a bell on his tablet to signal that students can begin their explanations. The teacher walks quickly around the groups listening for descriptions of the pictures as he goes. He stops to help a student get started by pointing to the eyes and asking what they are and whether both the man and the baby have them. He moves on as the partners start discussing other things that both the man and the baby have in common. The students quickly explain the similarities, but some partners forget to circle their photo when they agree on their answers, so the teacher reminds them to circle the similarities after their conversation.

After all the partners have circled a few similarities, the teacher once again gets the students' attention. He asks them to explain to their partner how the man and baby are different and circle those parts of the photo in red. The students notice things like leg length and wrinkles to explain the difference between the baby and the man.

When the students have finished, the teacher then says:

Now that you have identified how a baby and father are similar but not the same, let's do the same with the picture of the baby oak, called a **sapling**, and a mature oak tree. This time I want you to work with the person across from you, your across partner. To start the discussion, I want the person closest to me to go first.

The teacher then walks around as he did before, listening and intervening only to get partners back on track.

Elementary Nonexample of Partner Discussions

This teacher has the same learning target and also prepares photos for the lesson but hits a roadblock when giving directions. This teacher has tried asking his students to talk with partners in the past, but without much success. He does not have routines in place for smooth student interactions. When it comes time for directions, he simply says:

> I want you and your partner to talk about what is the same and different about the baby and the man that you can see in the photo.

Given the lack of routines for who will talk first and how to appropriately listen, one student in most groups takes the lead and talks during the entire time the teacher gives them to discuss. Routines are key to effective partner discussions. Without established routines, groups are usually not as effective as they could be.

Secondary Example of Partner Discussions

This example is from seventh-grade math in which the learning target is: *know the formulas for the circumference of a circle and use it to solve problems* (CCSS Math 7.G.4). The lesson is focused on teaching students the formula of a circumference. The teacher partners the students and designates A and B partners. Here is how she begins the lesson:

> The distance around a circle is called the **circumference**. Partner A, demonstrate for Partner B where the circumference of your circle is for Partner B. Partner B, give Partner A a thumbs-up if you agree. If you don't agree, show them what you think the circumference is, and then come to an agreement by asking the partners near you.

The teacher pauses and watches as students do this. She continues to explain:

> The distance through a circle at its center is called its **diameter**. Remember that we already talked about the diameter, and the diameter of a circle is twice as long as the radius. Partner B, show Partner A where the diameter is on the circle. Partner A, give Partner B a thumbs-up if you agree. If you don't agree, show your partner what you think is the diameter, and then come to an agreement by asking the partners near you.

The teacher pauses and watches as students do this. She then continues:

> The formula for the circumference of a circle is: $C = \pi \times d$, where $\pi = 3.14$. Partner A, state what you think the C stands for in the formula. *<pause>* Partner B, state what you think the d stands for in the formula. *<pause>*

The teacher once again listens and observes as partners interact. The teacher continues this process for the remainder of the lesson: presenting a sentence or two of critical content, and then asking students to demonstrate this content to their partners.

Secondary Nonexample of Partner Discussions

The nonexample teacher has the same learning target and explains the same critical content but does not feel that her students can interact with each other responsibly. So, when asking the questions, the teacher expects students to answer silently in their heads rather than responding to partners. Her approach deprives students of opportunities to share their thinking and hear what other students are thinking during their learning.

Determining If Students Can Engage in a Partner Discussion

As your students discuss critical content with partners, walk around and listen. Notice trends in student thinking. In addition to noticing whether students are talking to their partners, be sure to assess the content of their discussions. Students need to use academic language to discuss their thinking and perspectives about the critical content. If you do not get to all of the groups, ask the groups you missed to share their answers with the whole class.

Some suggestions for helping you know if students are effectively engaged in partner discussions include:

- Listen for specific academic language related to the critical content.

- Resist talking to groups; listen to the interaction without interfering.

- Read over students' shoulders if you have asked them to write during the discussion.

- Call on students you did not hear when partners were discussing to share with the class so you can hear their thinking.

Table 1.1 is a student proficiency scale for partner discussions that you can use and adapt as necessary to determine how students are progressing in their ability to engage in productive partner discussions.

Table 1.1: Student Proficiency Scale for Partner Discussions

Emerging	Fundamental	Desired Result
Students talk about the critical content. Students listen as their partners talk about the critical content.	Students share their perspective of the critical content. Students listen and respond as their partners discuss their perspective of the critical content.	Students actively discuss multiple perspectives of the critical content, listening to each other and adding onto each other's ideas.

Scaffold and Extend Instruction to Meet Students' Needs

Despite your best-laid plans, partner discussions are not always as beneficial as you would like them to be. You may need to scaffold or extend this technique to target the specific needs of some students.

Scaffolding

Some suggestions for scaffolding include:

- If there are students who struggle with reading, have students read to each other.

- Use a bulletin board to list ideas for students who may not know what to say. You may also choose to tape a copy of the chart to student desks for easier access. Figure 1.3 is a sample to use or adapt.

Figure 1.3: Anchor Chart for Partner Discussions

1. Restate what your partner said.

2. Add to what your partner said.

3. Be specific.

4. Explain why you think that.

5. Ask questions.

6. Explain what may make your thinking incorrect.

Extending

Some suggestions for extending include:

- Ask students to explain to their partners the connection between the critical content they are discussing and the unit as a whole.

- Ask students to create questions that would help other students discuss the critical content.

- Have students explain perspectives that differ from their own.

Instructional Technique 2

GROUPING FOR ACTIVE PROCESSING

Grouping students for active processing is the act of facilitating groups of students to interact with the content and with each other in meaningful ways as they learn. The College and Career Readiness Standard for Speaking and Listening, Standard 1, states that students must prepare for and participate effectively in a range of conversations and collaborations with diverse partners, building on others' ideas and expressing their own clearly and persuasively (Common Core State Standards Initiative, 2010). The ability to discuss and collaborate with partners is a skill all students need to learn to be ready to meet the challenges of college and career. Student interaction can enhance processing of content because it allows students to understand others' perspectives about the content. Group discussions not only allow students to hear other students' processing of information, but also it allows them to experience other students' reactions to their processing of content (Marzano, 2007).

How to Effectively Implement Grouping for Active Processing

The effective implementation of grouping for active processing uses the same set of steps in the introduction and demonstrated in the effective implementation of the first technique. As you read, note the adjustments and enhancements you will make to effectively implement grouping for this second technique—active processing.

Identify Critical Content

The purpose of this second technique is to provide opportunities for students to actively process critical content, thereby increasing the likelihood that they will understand and remember what you have taught. During direct instruction, break the content into smaller parts and plan to periodically stop to allow groups to actively process the content during the course of your instruction.

Make sure the chunk of content is "chewable." A chewable chunk is one that contains enough content for students to grapple with ideas and discuss different perspectives, yet not so large that students get lost or confused during the discussion. You want the chunk to be large enough to make it worth students' efforts to interact with a partner, but not so large that they fail to discuss all aspects of it in a short amount of time.

Plan a Meaningful Task

After identifying the critical content you want students to learn, decide how you will direct them to process the new information. Ideally, they will have multiple opportunities to process new content as a lesson progresses. Do not wait until the end of the lesson when students' working memories are overloaded with information or they sense that the lesson is over and are on to the next class or activity.

There are many options for processing new information, with summarizing and elaborating being just two of the most essential processing tasks. Think specifically of the prompts you will provide and what you will expect as responses from your students. The purpose of this technique is to help students think aloud, take a particular personal perspective on the content, and then hear other perspectives to more deeply process the content. Taking a perspective involves understanding how a situation appears to other students and inferring what the reasons might be for their cognitive and emotional reactions (Marzano & Heflebower, 2012). Help your students to do this. Plan to have them summarize, clarify, and predict as part of your instruction time. The time you allocate to active processing in groups will pay rich dividends when your students are able to immediately begin their assignments without frustration and confusion. These kinds of results are possible only when students have time to think about what they are learning and opportunities to ask their questions in the middle of an instructional sequence. Therefore, the prompts you provide are critical. There are four common subcomponents of effective grouping for active processing. These four subcomponents are all student actions: 1) summarizing and note taking, 2) representing knowledge nonlinguistically, 3) asking questions, and 4) reflecting on learning.

Focus your own questions, prompts, and directions on these four subcomponents to create meaningful tasks that allow students to process their thinking during instruction.

Structure Intentional Interactions

Now that you know what you want students to learn and the topic or task you want them to talk about as they actively process, the time has come to plan how you want students to interact. This technique lends itself to more informal conversations, but informality does not imply lack of structure. Plan how students will interact to respond to your prompts. Carefully map out the most basic routines such as who will begin the conversation and how turns will be taken. One way to structure student interaction during active processing is to number the desks the same in each group. When you call out a number, the student with that number in each group becomes the speaker. Figure 2.1 displays an example of what numbered seats would look like for an average-size class.

Figure 2.1: Sample Numbered Seats for Active Processing

1	2
3	4

1	2
3	4

1	2
3	4

1	2
3	4

1	2
3	4

1	2
3	4

If there is one correct answer, all other students in the group can agree or disagree and discuss. If the question calls for an open-ended response, other students can add to or adapt the original response. You might implement a round robin discussion in which the student to the left (or right) of the student who began the discussion takes a turn, and then the conversation continues around the circle. Think ahead to anticipate all of the exceptions to any rule (different numbers of students in groups, students who will need support) before you implement the technique in class.

Team (or shared) whiteboards can also be used as a variation for how students will respond and interact. This approach requires that students collaborate to determine a team answer to the questions you pose. If you use this method, establish routines to ensure that one student is not doing all the work. One example could include setting a recurring timer and rotating the whiteboard and the marker to another student whenever the timer buzzes. Another variation is to ask one specific student to act as the scribe. Take care to designate a student who will be willing to listen to other students' ideas.

Other variations include:

- Make collaborative posters on which students in a group write their responses on a piece of chart paper using different colored marker to distinguish their responses from each other (Fisher & Frey, 2014).

- Make team statements in which each student contributes an individual statement, and then the team as a whole comes to an agreement about a summarizing statement that incorporates the various views.

- Place mats, such as the one shown in Figure 2.2, are helpful for organizing team statements. The place mat allows four students to each write in their own sections located along the outside edge of the mat with space for a team statement to be written in the middle.

Figure 2.2: Team Place Mat

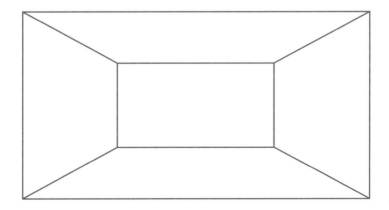

Organize Students Into Groups

Now that you have decided how your students will interact to process content, think about how to organize the groups. Long-term groups work best when students have had previous opportunities to work together. Consider reorganizing student groups every month or at the beginning of every new unit. If you teach at the elementary level, consider creating different groups for different subjects so that students can work with a variety of partners during each school day. Groups of two to five work best. Consider students' strengths and weaknesses as well as any personal histories they may have with other students. One easy way to group students is to write each student's name on an index card at the start of the school year. This allows you to easily sort your students into groups. You can quickly shift students between groups without erasing or forgetting any students. An efficient way to do this is to create columns of groups so you can quickly see that each column contains the correct number of students. Using your index cards to group students into columns also allows you to create a row of "talkers," "creative thinkers," or any other subgroup of student strengths that you want to spread out among groups. If you teach middle or high school, index cards can be a quick way to show students their new seat assignments. You can place the index cards on student desks so that when they walk into class, they can quickly find their new seat.

Establish Routines

Students will not automatically understand the rules and procedures that apply to group work, so early on establish rules and procedures that are specific to active processing. Explain the relevant rules and procedures to your students the first time you use this technique. You might think about posting the rules in a prominent place in your classroom so you and your students can refer to them when you implement this technique. Here are some ideas of expectations for students that you might post:

- State your own perspective.

- Be respectful of the perspectives of others.

- Make sure you understand.

- Be willing to answer other group members.

If you want your students to sit in their groups as a new seating arrangement, consider the routines of how you will help them quickly become accustomed to this new organization. If possible, organize the desks or tables ahead of time so that as students come into class, the arrangement will be ready for interaction. If you decide to number the desks to help with the organization of who speaks when, have the numbers affixed on the desks beforehand.

If your students will not be sitting with their groups throughout the lesson, think about routines you want to establish for quick transitions into other groups. Think about how students will physically move to their appointed areas. Ensure that groups have established places in the room that allow them to see and hear all members in their group.

Teach and Reinforce Conative Skills

No matter how much time you spend planning for "perfect" groups and routines, you will experience glitches along the way. The discussion between group members can become heated or, in some cases, students will just drop out of the discussion and refuse to participate. The best way to circumvent those issues is to teach your students what responsible interaction looks like. Discuss and model assertive communication so they understand examples and nonexamples of effective, responsible interaction. Ask two students who are strong communicators to model what productive academic conversations look and sound like while you highlight what they are doing well. If possible, resist correcting students so as not to discourage them from volunteering in the future.

Help your students understand that disagreeing with a peer is not a negative behavior, per se. The way in which the disagreement plays out can create either a positive or negative experience. Be patient with your students, and plan to redirect, model, and give frequent feedback to them.

Common Mistakes

Any time you implement a new technique, the first few attempts may feel awkward. Your students will not instantly be effective at working with each other to actively process content. They will need multiple interactions until they acquire the skills they need for responsible interaction. You will also need time to learn how to facilitate student groups more effectively. Plan ahead to avoid the following common mistakes as you begin to help your student groups actively process.

- The teacher fails to focus the active processing on the critical content.

- The teacher asks students to restate content rather than process it.

- The teacher does not model or facilitate effective processing.

- The teacher allows students to discuss topics other than critical content.

Examples and Nonexamples of Grouping for Active Processing in the Classroom

As you think about your implementation of active processing, consider the following classroom examples and nonexamples. While reading these, keep in mind the common mistakes mentioned previously. Note how the example teachers avoid them and the nonexample teachers miss the mark by making one or more of these mistakes.

Elementary Example of Grouping for Active Processing

In this first classroom example, the learning target is: *analyze and interpret data from maps to describe patterns of Earth's features* (NGSS 4-ESS2-2). The fourth-grade teacher knows that to achieve that goal, the first step is teaching her students how to identify features on maps. To that end, the teacher collects several types of maps that contain the features she will teach: mountains, continental boundaries, and volcanoes. She instructs students to create a table with three rows and two columns in their notebooks and tells them to title the left column *feature* and the right column *how I know*. The teacher frequently uses place mats as a way to facilitate active processing. She has laminated place mats for each group of four and provides whiteboard markers and erasers.

She first shows several examples of mountains on different types of maps but does not tell students what they are. She reminds students not to call out answers, even if they think they know what feature she is demonstrating. After she shows all of the examples, she continues the lesson:

Not all maps look alike, and you will need to be able to iden-tify this feature on different types of maps, so make sure you describe its defining characteristics. Now that you have seen several examples of this feature, I want you to answer two questions: What is the feature? and How can you tell? When you think about how you can tell, write your answer on your part of the place mat. After everyone in your group is finished writing, I want you to share your answers, and then agree upon a way to identify this feature on maps in the future. When you all agree, write how to identify mountains on maps in the center of your place mat.

The teacher then walks around reading what students are writing and lis-tens as students come to agreements about how they can identify mountains on maps. When the students finish, the teacher asks a few groups to tell the whole class what they placed in the center of their place mats. The teacher then asks students to record how to identify mountains in the table they cre-ated in their notebooks. She asks students to wipe off their place mats and follow the same procedure for the next two features: continental boundaries and volcanoes.

Elementary Nonexample of Grouping for Active Processing

The nonexample teacher posts the two questions: What is the feature? and How can you tell? She then has students quietly write their responses in their notebooks, and then tell each other what they wrote. There is no expec-tation that students will provide feedback to their peers about the accuracy of their answers, which forces the teacher to work much harder as she hurries around the room checking all the answers and redirecting students who are not correct in their initial responses.

Secondary Example of Grouping for Active Processing

It is early in the year in a middle school social studies class, and the teacher has students sitting in groups of four with numbered desks. She wants to begin teaching her students the learning target: *construct arguments using claims and evidence from multiple sources, while acknowledging the strengths and limitations of the arguments* (C3 Framework for Social Studies State Standards D4.1.6-8). To do this, she takes time to explicitly teach her students how to state a claim. She describes what a claim is and presents examples and non-examples. She then pauses and gives directions:

> Now that you have heard what makes an effective claim, restate the definition or description in your own words. Student number one at each table, go first and summarize what I said for your tablemates. Then, each student needs to either add to the summary or ask a question to help clarify what makes an effective claim. When all of you are finished, student number four, write a sentence on your whiteboard explaining this step.

The teacher sets the timer for two minutes and walks around listening for summaries of her description of a claim. She reads the whiteboards at the end of the two minutes, pointing out unique ways students described how to effectively state a claim. The teacher now has clear knowledge of which students understand the mechanics of how to state a claim. Armed with this information, the teacher targets those students who need additional help while other students begin to state a claim independently.

Secondary Nonexample of Grouping for Active Processing

The teacher in this nonexample is focused on the same content, stating a claim. Instead of stopping periodically and asking students to discuss chunks of the lesson with their peers, she rushes through the information in the interest of saving time. She then moves immediately to having students practice together stating a claim. Since some students have never been asked to state a claim in the past, there is considerable confusion and as a result the teacher ends up reteaching much of what she went over, therefore not saving time at all.

Determining If Students Can Actively Process Critical Content

Listen to student conversations to assess whether they are actively processing critical content. Here are some suggestions for monitoring students' interactions:

- Circulate and listen to student interactions. As you work with a group, listen to students while you scan the room for other distractions. Conversations can be rich, and you may be tempted to be drawn into lengthy discussions. Remember that your role is to make sure that students are actively processing. If students are misguided in their discussion, steer them back on track and move on. Circle back around soon to check that they maintained their focus, keeping in mind that you cannot stay with one group for any length of time.

- Read over students' shoulders as they write on their place mats. Notice if the information is accurate and focused on the critical content.

- Have students complete their group poster on a wall so that you can quickly scan the statements and check for accuracy.

Use the student proficiency scale found in Table 2.1 to help you gauge whether your students are achieving the desired results.

Table 2.1: Student Proficiency Scale for Grouping for Active Processing

Emerging	Fundamental	Desired Result
Students talk about content.	Students summarize, elaborate, and reflect on accurate content.	Students actively participate in a discussion in which they summarize, elaborate, and reflect on accurate content.
Students listen as other students talk about content.	Students listen and respond as other students process content.	Students listen to and add on to each other's statements. Students can explain how their understanding of critical content has changed due to interacting with their peers to actively process.

Scaffold and Extend Instruction to Meet Students' Needs

Not all of your student groups will be able to actively process consistently. There will also be students within some of the groups who struggle with processing in general. Through monitoring, identify those two groups of students as well as students who are able to quickly process critical content in their groups. Following are suggestions for scaffolding and extending this technique to meet the needs of your students.

Scaffolding

Here are some suggestions for scaffolding the grouping for active processing:

- Give a specific number of tokens or paperclips to each student in the group. Each time students talk, they put a token in the middle of the table. This accounting system allows students to know precisely how many times they can and should contribute to a discussion. When their tokens are all in the middle, they cannot contribute again until everyone else has used all their tokens. Giving students tokens allows them to be aware of how often they contribute to a conversation. This adaptation can help your students who contribute too much or too little to their groups. A more visual version of this is to use colored chips so that you have a visual representation of which students might be dominating or not contributing to the conversation.

- Provide sentence stems to students or groups that are not quick to work together to actively process the content. Following is a list to copy and leave at the desk of students who need help to converse with each other about content to summarize, elaborate, and reflect:

  - I agree with you and want to add . . .

  - My idea is slightly different. I think . . .

  - I thought the answer was _____. Can you help me?

  - Why do you think that?

  - Can you explain that to me?

  - Let me see if I understand. You're saying . . .

    — My idea is slightly different . . .

    — Here's something we might try . . .

Extending

For students who actively process in groups without much effort, plan ahead for how you will extend their learning by selecting one of the following options or creating your own extensions:

- Ask students to identify the pros and cons of their personal perspectives.

- Ask students to explain how the critical content they are learning relates to the unit as a whole.

- Ask students to be the first (or last) person in their groups to share, since those positions in the group are usually more difficult, depending on the question.

Instructional Technique 3

PAIRED PRACTICE

Paired practice is a technique in which one student practices a skill, strategy, or process and a partner provides coaching feedback and advice. The roles reverse frequently. The advantage of paired practice is that students have multiple opportunities to see and hear the thinking processes of their peers as they practice a skill. Paired practice also allows students to experience alternate ways of executing a procedure.

The next natural step to the gradual release model of "I do, we do, you do" is "I do, we do, you do together, you do alone" (Frey, Fisher & Everlove, 2009). When you add paired practice as the "you do together" step, students who need more guidance will have additional opportunities to learn. In addition, you will have a window of time to step back and more closely observe your class. At that point, you can more readily identify those students who need further support. Adding the technique of paired practice to the gradual release model will enable you to be more timely in your instructional decisions regarding scaffolding and/or extending your instruction.

How to Effectively Implement Paired Practice

Paired practice uses the same set of steps described in the introduction and previous two techniques. The goal of paired practice is for students to increase their proficiency in demonstrating a skill, strategy, or process. Read each step with that goal in mind.

Identify Critical Content

The first step in the implementation of paired practice is to identify the critical content of the skill, strategy, or process that the student pairs will practice. Break the skill, strategy, or process into specific pieces of critical content for students to practice and master with their partners.

Plan a Meaningful Task

The next step is to determine what you will ask students to do during their paired practice. Think about which aspects of the procedural knowledge you want students to practice with their partners. Short practice sessions with frequent interaction can be more powerful than expecting students to practice a long, complicated procedure. If the procedure has multiple steps, have students practice in pairs for each step separately. They will then be able to focus on the critical content of each step and receive specific feedback from their partners.

Structure Intentional Interactions

Next, plan for how students will interact with each other during the paired practice session. If two students are left unmonitored, one student may often do all of the work, leaving the other student to either watch or totally disengage. The interaction should unfold in the following sequence. First, one student works on the skill, strategy, or process while the other student observes. Then, the observing student gives feedback. Partners check each other's work for accuracy and discuss their personal approach to the activity. Students give their partners feedback on what part of the procedure they performed accurately, as well as note areas for growth. If students do not know how to solve a problem or complete the process, they should still attempt it, listen to feedback, and write down what they learn.

When first implementing paired practice, guide students to prevent one student from monopolizing the interaction. The purpose of this technique is for both students to practice. Students do not have to know the answer to be the one writing. The purpose of paired practice is two brains working together to practice one skill.

Think about the logistics of which student will write first and how long you will give the partners to explain their thinking. Determine in advance how you will facilitate individual accountability. Individual student mini-whiteboards work well for this strategy because you can readily see students' thinking and they can quickly erase and change their responses as their thinking changes. Not all practice needs to be recorded for students to later review, but students might find it useful to copy down the last example they practice for each chunk of critical content so they have an example to refer to when they are independently practicing.

A variation of paired practice is Share and Compare in which, after the team practices, they join a neighboring group to become a group of four. Students compare their answers with the other group and revise any discrepancies they find. This variation helps ensure accuracy and allows students to hear multiple perspectives.

Organize Students Into Groups

Now that you have decided what and how students will practice, plan how you will organize your students into pairs. Assigning pairs should be purposeful and somewhat fluid. Many factors go into a perfect partner pairing. Quite often teachers group knowledgeable students with struggling students or compliant students with students who do not always follow the rules. In addition to thinking about students' knowledge or behavior when grouping students, also consider factors such as work ethic, leadership skills, and relationships. Leverage the emotional side of learning to enhance your partner groups. For example, consider the following:

- Partner a quiet student with a student who asks questions rather than taking charge.

- Pair a very knowledgeable student with a more creative student.

- Partner two students who are struggling if they struggle with different aspects of the content or cooperative learning.

- Partner natural leaders to work with students who need guidance and patient instruction.

- Pair students who have similar strengths with each other, so they can feed off one another and extend their thinking in ways you had not planned.

Establish Routines

Along with planning what, how, and with whom students will practice, consider the routines students will need to have a smooth session of paired practice. Clear communication entails explicit instruction of the expectations for the routine, modeling of those expectations, and opportunities for students to practice those routines. For example, explain specifically what action you want from students after you signal. Model for students what that action looks like. Ask students to practice that action a few times so you can check their understanding of the routine.

Here is a list of routines you might want to implement:

- Who, where, and how to get supplies (i.e., mini-whiteboard and markers)

- Where to meet with their partners

- Signals

  - Start talking

  - Change speaker

  - Stop talking

- How to regroup in case of absent partners

When you create partner groups, plan to change your seating plan so that partners are near one another. If that is not possible, ensure that there is a clear path to their meeting place to ease and speed up transitions.

Teach and Reinforce Conative Skills

Paired practice can be emotionally tricky for some students because they are expected to make their work and thinking available to a peer who will give them feedback. There is a measure of risk for students, especially if they have not experienced peer feedback. In the average classroom, few students risk thinking out loud. They do not answer questions unless they are confident that they are correct. In this technique, you are asking students to formulate their thoughts and then think aloud in front of a peer. Plan how you will support your students as they take these risks. Resiliency is a critical conative skill. Facilitate and support it in your classroom. Here are just a few ways you might do this:

- Build relationships with your students.

- Seek out the more reticent students and initiate informal conversations with them about nonthreatening topics such as music, sports, or popular culture.

- Communicate and demonstrate to all students your belief in their abilities to learn.

- Support students as they struggle through challenging problems.

- Give students hints or ask guiding questions rather than give students the answer.

- Establish group routines so all students not only expect to participate but also know that their contributions will be valued.

Another important conative skill to foster in your students is the avoidance of negative thinking. Help students become aware of negative thoughts and emotions and specific situations in which they tend to arise. Once students are aware of their negative thinking, the next step is to help them avoid it by helping them to monitor their internal dialogues and reframe their statements to self. You might prompt them with statements and questions such as the following:

- What is the worst that could happen?

- How likely is that to happen?

- Take a few minutes to think things through.

- Is that what you feel or what you think? (Marzano, 2013)

Common Mistakes

There are several common ways that teachers can derail paired practice and decrease students' benefit from this technique.

- The teacher fails to provide opportunities for students to attempt the practice individually before partner practice.

- The teacher uses paired practice for students to check answers rather than discuss a skill, strategy, or process.

- The teacher does not structure student interactions that provide students with opportunities to discuss their personal approaches to an activity.

- The teacher asks student to practice procedures that are lengthy, leaving little time for interaction.

Examples and Nonexamples of Paired Practice

Following are two sets of examples and corresponding nonexamples (one elementary and one secondary) showing how paired practice can be used in classrooms. As you read these examples, note the components of effective implementation described earlier and the common mistakes just listed.

Elementary Example of Paired Practice

In this elementary example, the lesson is preparing the student to demonstrate the learning target: *use multiplication and division to solve word problems* (CCSS.Math.3.OA.3). The third-grade teacher has already modeled various ways to solve word problems using multiplication and division and given students opportunities to discuss the different methods she modeled. She has manipulatives available for students should they need them. The students have different partners for math than they do in other subjects, so the teacher begins the practice session by asking them to pair up with their math buddies.

> Class, it's time to practice what we just learned. I want each partner to work the same problem independently. After each of you has solved the problem, compare your answers. If you got different answers, talk about how each one solved the problem and together decide whether someone made a mistake. If you got the same answers but solved the problem differently, explain to each other how you solved it. If you solved the problem in the same way, work together to come up with another way to solve the problem.

The teacher has these steps written on the board.

1. Solve the problem independently

2. Show your partner

   - Different answers—look for mistakes

   - Same answers, different way of solving—explain each way

   - Same answer, same way of solving—find another way to solve

I will walk around to help you if you get stuck and also to talk with you about how confident you feel about solving word problems. When you are confident, you can return to your desk and work by yourself. Partner A, pick up two copies of the practice sheet. Partner B, grab any objects or other supplies you think you and your partner might need to solve these problem. After you have your materials, head to your work spot.

As the students transition to their math buddy locations, the teacher redirects and ensures that the transition is quick, and all students begin work immediately. The teacher then listens to make sure students are practicing multiple ways to solve the problems. As students gain confidence, she releases them to work independently, sometime rearranging buddies for students who need additional paired practice with another partner.

Elementary Nonexample of Paired Practice

In this nonexample, the teacher uses the same practice sheets and introduces the lesson:

Class, it's time to practice what we just learned. I want you to do some problems with your math buddy so that you can be confident about solving problems like these independently. I want you both to work the problems independently, showing how you came up with your answers. When you are both done solving the problems, show each other your answers. If you got different answers, work together to decide whose answer is correct. Partner A, come get two copies of the practice sheet. Partner B, grab any objects or other supplies you think you and your partner might need to solve these problems. After you have your materials, head to your work spot.

The students then silently work through the practice problems, and when they are done with the sheet, they share with their partners and decide who is right.

The lack of chunking of paired practice ends up creating a situation in which students may practice their incorrect way of solving the problem many times before getting feedback that they are making a mistake. The nonexample teacher's approach also results in some students needlessly spending time practicing because they are already able to solve problems using multiplication and division.

Secondary Example of Paired Practice

The learning target students are practicing in this lesson is: *introduce precise, knowledgeable claim(s)* (CCSS ELA & Literacy, Writing Standard 6-12, Grades 11-12). The teacher notices in her students' writing samples that while most students are already competent and confident in their ability to introduce claims, the class as a whole needs additional practice on being precise and knowledgeable in their statements. Because of this, she plans to spend class time on this isolated skill. The teacher models what a precise, knowledgeable claim looks like and has students compare examples and nonexamples of claims. The class is reading *Song of Myself* by Walt Whitman. For students to practice making their claims, the teacher poses the question: Do you identify with Walt Whitman, or do you find yourself resisting his attempts to pull you into his way of thinking? All students have copies of the poem to use for reference, and they sit in pairs.

She continues with the lesson:

> Class, now that you have spent time discussing your answers to this question with your partner, I want you to state your claim on a whiteboard. Remember that we are just practicing writing claims. Do not try to write the entire essay on your whiteboard. Remember, today's focus is on making your claim precise and knowledgeable.

Students spend a few minutes writing their claims on the whiteboard.

> Now I want you to read over each other's claims. When you do, I want you to underline words that are precise and circle the part of the claim that shows the writer (your partner) is knowledgeable about the poem. Some of the claims may be both circled and underlined because they show that your partner is both precise and knowledgeable. Then, take turns giving your partner some suggestions about how to improve their statement.

As the students do this, the teacher walks around helping students find the precise and knowledgeable sections and offering suggestions for growth.

> Now that you've gotten some feedback, I want you to revise your claims. Go into more detail and use more precise language. Then share your new statement with your partner.

As students revise and share, the teacher once again walks around looking and listening to make sure students are discussing how to make precise, knowledgeable claims.

> Now that you have a feel for how to do this, let's practice once more. This time, I want you to write another response to this question, cite different reasons, and use different information to support it. You can change your position if you prefer, but either way, you need to use different justifications than you used before.

The class then follows the same process as before for feedback and revision.

Secondary Nonexample of Paired Practice

Instead of asking students to attempt the claim on their own first and then share with a partner, the nonexample teacher simply tells students to work in pairs to state a claim. The partner groups then show their claims to the whole class, and the teacher comments on each of the groups' claims, resulting in much of the class time being spent on the teacher giving feedback rather than the students getting to practice and receiving feedback from their peers.

Determining If Students Can Effectively Practice in Pairs

As students are working, check for evidence of the desired result in their work products. Determine if students are enhancing their learning due to paired practice and also whether all students are growing and learning as a result of the technique.

- Move quickly about the room, catching snippets of conversation here and there. If students are practicing accurately, keep moving. The point is that students practice and share how they are able to complete their procedure. If the pairs are practicing and sharing effectively, no need to intervene. Every moment that you are talking is a moment you are denying students opportunities to give or hear another student's perspective of how to practice skills, strategies, or processes. Furthermore, you are denying yourself the opportunity to ascertain if paired practice is effective.

- Periodically, ask students to hold up their mini-whiteboards so you can quickly scan for accuracy.

- Have students complete the last practice problem on an index card and turn it in so you can quickly sort the cards into three groups: students who understand how to complete the procedure correctly (even if there are simple mistakes), those who have minor misconceptions, and those who may need significant interventions.

Use the student proficiency scale for paired practice in Table 3.1 to help you know if students are achieving the desired result of this technique.

Table 3.1: Student Proficiency Scale for Paired Practice

Emerging	Fundamental	Desired Result
Students attempt the skill, strategy, or process.	Students explain the skill, strategy, or process they are practicing.	Students actively interact with each other to explore different accurate procedures for completing the skill, strategy, or process.
Students listen as other partner talks about the skill, strategy, or process.	Students watch and listen as their partner explains a procedure for completing the skill, strategy, or process.	Students successfully practice independently using multiple procedures discussed in paired practice.
Students attempt to execute procedures independently after paired practice.	Students practice independently using procedures discussed in paired practice.	

Scaffold and Extend Instruction to Meet Students' Needs

Plan ahead for adaptations you might make as your students are practicing in pairs. Following are some ways to both scaffold and extend your students' learning.

Scaffolding

- Provide graphic organizers for students who need more structure to their practice.

- Ask students to practice a specific aspect of the skill, strategy, or process rather than the entire process.

- Provide problems that are solved and ask students to explain the logic of the solutions.

Extending

- Ask students to demonstrate multiple methods for executing the skill, strategy, or process.

- Give students a problem that is solved incorrectly, and ask them to explain the error in logic and correct it.

- Ask students to create a "tips" page that could be used by other students as they practice the skill, strategy, or process.

Instructional Technique 4

STRUCTURED GROUPING

Your key role when implementing structured grouping is to provide students with both structure and accountability to complete a work product. Structured grouping works well when students are deepening their knowledge, because it allows them more time to work and requires them to apply what they are learning. Both individual and group accountability are prominently featured. Because there is an expected work product, structured grouping works most effectively with extending knowledge rather than processing new content. Thus, "productive group work is an essential stepping-stone to learning and mastery" (Fry, Fisher & Everlove, 2009, p. 14).

How to Effectively Implement Structured Grouping

There are six teacher behaviors to effectively implement structured grouping: 1) identifying critical content, 2) planning a meaningful task, 3) structuring intentional interaction, 4) organizing students into groups, 5) establishing routines for interacting, and 6) teaching and reinforcing conative skills.

Identify Critical Content

Because structured grouping works best when students are extending knowledge rather than processing new content, decide which critical content you want students to deepen. Then, plan what you want students to do to extend their knowledge. If you simply want students to discuss critical content, this is probably not the best technique. This technique lends itself to being paired with activities that ask students to examine similarities and differences, examine their reasoning, or other rigorous instructional strategies.

Plan a Meaningful Task

Based on the type of critical content you want students to focus on and what you want students to do with the critical content, choose or create a task for students to complete with their groups. The task should be manageable for students, but not easy. The rationale for using a meaningful task for structured grouping is that students should struggle productively to accomplish this task. When you use this technique with students for the first time, the tasks can and should be very structured. You can provide questions and even an organizer to help students complete their task. As you and your students become more adept with structured grouping, you can eventually provide an open-ended, cognitively complex question that requires students to work together and share their expertise to provide a detailed answer to the question.

This technique can be combined with instructional strategies such as helping students examine similarities and differences or examine their reasoning. As noted earlier, when two or more instructional strategies are combined, they become a macrostrategy. When you are looking for meaningful tasks for students to complete, look to other disciplines for inspiration.

Examples of meaningful tasks include:

- Students in groups compare ways they have learned to add numbers and create a guide for when each method is preferable.

- Students in groups analyze a video of a basketball lay-up, discussing and agreeing on strengths and possible areas of growth.

- Students in groups collaborate to revise their original prediction of how to best conserve water in the school cafeteria based on information they collected.

Structure Intentional Interactions

You have likely been a part of groups in which you were either the person who did all the work or the one who got out of all of the work. For all students to enhance their learning in groups, every student needs an assigned responsibility. Productive group work requires both individual and group accountability. For example, absent individual accountability, a completed task may demonstrate higher-level thinking, but it may not constitute evidence that every student participated in the process. As you plan how students will interact to complete the task, plan how all students in the group will demonstrate the learning target in their own unique ways. Asking all students to write an answer to the same question sometimes leads to one student doing the work and other students copying. Your time is better spent listening for accuracy and facilitating student groups to deepen their under-standing of critical content than checking that students are not copying each other's answers.

No matter what the task, build in time for students to think individually about the content before they share with peers. Individual think time allows students to examine their own thinking along with reinforcing individual accountability. Once students have individually processed the content, they then need time to share and hear other students' perspectives.

Provide group structures to ensure that all students have opportunities to hear the thinking of others and provide feedback. One way to do this is to provide a list of responsibilities necessary to complete the task. Students can then decide who completes which responsibility and understand how their responsibilities work together to demonstrate the critical content.

Some teachers accomplish these structures with more general roles instead of listing responsibilities specific to the task. Some roles include:

- The *discussion starter*, who asks guiding questions and ensures the discussion stays focused on critical content and task completion.

- The *facilitator*, who ensures that students participate equally by encouraging quiet students and helping active students allow others to talk.

- The *regulator*, who acts as timekeeper and ensures that the logistics, such as data collection, take place.

- The *elaborator*, who points out connections between responses and adds to other students' responses.

Figure 4.1 displays a set of cards to help students remember their roles. You can reproduce the cards and give them to individual students. When the activity is complete, collect the cards to be used for another time.

Figure 4.1: Student Roles for Structured Grouping

Discussion Starter

1. Ask questions to start the discussion.

2. Make sure the discussion stays on track.

3. Make sure the work gets done.

Facilitator

1. Make sure all group members participate equally.

2. Politely help all students get a turn to talk.

3. Ask questions of students who have not taken a turn to talk.

Regulator

1. Keep track of time.

2. Collect supplies if needed.

3. Document data if needed.

Elaborator

1. Add to what other students say.

2. Point out connections between answers.

3. Ask about differences between answers.

Variations of the structured group technique include:

- Perspective analysis (Marzano, 1992), in which there are five specific steps for students to scrutinize their own opinion as well as a contrasting opinion

- Parallel thinking (de Bono, 1999), in which students explore multiple perspectives on a topic by representing perspectives (wearing different colored hats) to discuss the topic

- Literature circles, in which the roles and questions are specific to text students are reading

Organize Students Into Groups

There are several ways to assign roles to students: 1) assign roles based on students' personalities or temperaments as you have observed them in your class, 2) have students choose the roles they want, 3) have students draw a role card from a bag. Mix up the way roles are determined to avoid repetitive role assignments.

If you decide to designate the roles, first place students into the role category you choose for them, and then group students so there is a representative for each role in each group. After your students have become accustomed to group work, give them a voice in the selection of their group members. To do this, ask each student to write the names of three classmates with whom they would like to work. Use that information to assign groups, ensuring that students gets at least one person from their lists in their groups. This process provides the perfect opportunity to discuss group skills with students, pointing out, for example, why their best friends may not be the best choices as fellow group members. Ask the class to brainstorm what makes someone a good group member, and then remind them of these traits when they are writing down their choices.

Establish Routines

Establish routines for the roles you will ask students to fill. Teach students the role. Model what the role entails, and ask students to summarize. Use a group as an example, explain each role using student names, and then allow a moment or two to let students in other groups identify the corresponding roles in their own groups before you explain the responsibilities of the roles. After you finish explaining the logistics, give students time to summarize what their roles are to their group members before starting the task.

Establish routines to require accountability and feedback on how students fulfilled the responsibilities of their roles. Role cards with blank spaces to fill in the responsibilities of each role might be helpful for this process. You can also establish a routine for the end of the activity, when students will report to their groups how they demonstrated the responsibilities of their roles.

Teach and Reinforce Conative Skills

As an adult, you automatically and constantly interpret situations, either pleasing or challenging, in which you find yourself. This same principle applies to students. As students work together in structured groups, they must become aware of the reality that they may interpret things differently than other group members do. Help students realize that differences in interpretation are not based on a rigid categorization of right and wrong but rather on what various group members think, feel, and believe.

Viewing a situation or an issue from multiple perspectives is a skill that is essential for understanding and interacting with others. Do not expect that students will necessarily know how to execute that conative skill. Model it, remind students about it, and frequently talk about what is critical about this skill. Keep the skill of sharing perspectives in the forefront every time you ask your students to interact until they demonstrate proficiency with stating their own perspectives and analyzing the perspectives of others.

Common Mistakes

As you implement structured grouping with your students, you will undoubtedly encounter some roadblocks. Here are some common mistakes to watch out for and plan ahead to avoid:

- The teacher fails to require cognitively complex thinking from students during the completion of their task.

- The teacher fails to provide appropriate structures for student interactions such that students either do not interact with one another toward the goal of group accountability or "divide and conquer" the task.

- The teacher fails to structure individual accountability so there is no evidence of what each student contributed to the thinking and completion of the work product.

- The teacher fails to facilitate responsible interaction and sharing perspectives through routines, modeling, and feedback.

Examples and Nonexample of Structured Grouping

Following are two sets of examples and nonexamples (one elementary and one secondary) showing how teachers implement the structured grouping technique. As you read, imagine how this technique might look in your classroom. Notice that one example divides responsibilities, while the other assigns roles. In both examples, all students need to demonstrate the learning target.

Elementary Example of Structured Grouping

The learning target for the lesson is: *compare and contrast the point of view from which different stories are narrated, including the difference between first- and third-person narrations* (CCSS Reading for Literacy K–5, 4th grade). To help her students acquire this skill, the teacher uses two stories with differing points of view that students have already read. The class uses a routine in which student desks have four different symbols, one on each desk in the group of four: moon, sun, star, and cloud.

On the board, the teacher writes the following responsibilities:

> Moon and Star: Find evidence of how the narration is the same in the two stories.

> Sun and Cloud: Find evidence of how the narration is different in the two stories.

> Class, today each group is going to look at how the points of view in these two stories are the same and different. To do this, each of you will have your own responsibility in the activity. The responsibilities are listed on the board. Notice that you have the same responsibility as someone else in your group. I want each of you to find your own evidence in the stories. Please work by yourself to start. I will give you ten minutes to find as much evidence as you can. Use your sticky notes to mark the spot, and write how the narration is the same or different on that sticky note so you can remember.

The teacher then sets a timer and walks around to observe what students are writing on their sticky notes. She pauses periodically to assist or help a student find evidence. When the timer goes off, the teacher says:

> Now that you all have found some evidence, I want you to take turns presenting that evidence in your groups. Present in the same order that is shown on the board: Moon, Star, Sun, Cloud. After the first two students share their evidence, as a group, discuss and agree on evidence of how the narrations are the same. Everyone in the group needs to write this evidence on their papers. Then, do the same thing after the second two students in your group share their evidence.

As students complete this activity, the teacher walks around looking and listening to make sure students share their evidence and responsibly communicate as they agree upon appropriate evidence in the stories for how the narrations in the two stories are similar and different.

Elementary Nonexample of Structured Grouping

In this nonexample, the teacher expects students to complete the same activity with their groups, but fails to assign responsibilities. Some groups work well together and discuss evidence as they find it, and some students simply work independently, not interacting with their peers at all. The failure to assign responsibilities to students ahead of time results in time wasted and many disengaged students.

Secondary Example of Structured Grouping

The learning target for this world history class is: *analyze complex and interacting factors that influenced the perspectives of people during different historical eras* (C3 Framework for Social Studies State Standards D2.His.4.9-12). Previous lessons in this example classroom have focused on aspects of World War I (WWI) and World War II (WWII), including the economic and social conditions during those periods. For students to demonstrate this learning target, the teacher supplies them with two editorials, one written during each war, and reads them aloud to the class. She also gives students time to annotate the editorials, documenting evidence of factors that influenced the perspectives of people during those times. Students have used and are familiar with the role cards: Discussion Starter, Facilitator, Regulator,

Elaborator. To begin the activity, the teacher places the role cards upside down on each table of four and states:

> In your groups, you are going to analyze how these editorials appear to be influenced by the economic and social conditions during the period of time each was written. To do that, I want you to each draw a card at your table to determine which role you will fulfill during your discussion. Draw your card and talk with your group about your responsibilities so everyone is clear about their individual responsibility during the discussion. Then take a few minutes to prepare for your role. Once everyone in your group is ready, begin your discussion. Make sure you are citing evidence from the editorials and using information you have learned about the conditions during each of those wars. I want to see everyone referring back to their notes and using their textbooks to support the discussion.

The teacher listens to the discussions, reminding students of the responsibilities of their roles, helping students analyze the influential factors, and prompting them to document evidence that is discussed. When conversations appear to have run their course, the teacher instructs all students to answer the original prompt in their academic notebooks, citing evidence from the editorials that they discussed in their groups.

Secondary Nonexample of Structured Grouping

The following nonexample is based on the same learning target. The teacher provides the same editorials, directions, and roles. However, when the time arrives for students to discuss, the teacher sits with one group during the entire allotted time to discuss the evidence with them. The other groups soon realize that they are not going to be held accountable for their group interactions. Many students silently complete the assignment or noisily chat about nonacademic topics.

Determining If Structured Grouping Enhances Student Learning

To determine if structured grouping enhances student learning, do more than just visually check to see whether one student in each group is talking. Monitor students in real time to assess whether they are growing and learning in their groups. Circle back to each group several times so you can hear different students speak. You might also set up a system for students to check in with you as they work together. This way you can intentionally ensure the desired result is occurring as students are working and also discover when a group is on the wrong track or is not productive in advance of the due date for the work product. Here are some ways to monitor your students during structured grouping:

- Listen to group interactions to ensure that students are taking responsibility for adhering to the roles assigned.

- Ask the regulators to summarize the progress on the task and listen to ensure all students have participated.

- Look over the task and ask students questions about different sections.

- Ask students to initial their contributions and look for everyone's initials.

Table 4.1 is a student proficiency scale for structured grouping that can be used or adapted to determine how students are progressing in their ability to work productively in a structured group.

Table 4.1: Student Proficiency Scale for Structured Grouping

Emerging	Fundamental	Desired Result
Students perform their role or responsibility.	Students actively participate in completing the task.	Students interact responsibly and equally to complete the task.
Students allow group mates to perform their roles or responsibilities.	Students listen to others and discuss their own understanding of the critical content.	Students can explain how their understanding and the understanding of their group mates are similar and different.
		Students can explain how they and their group mates contributed to the task.

Scaffold and Extend Instruction to Meet Students' Needs

As you become more skilled in facilitating structured groups in your classroom, you will often identify students who need more support or students who need permission to move ahead. Use the following scaffolds and extensions to better meet the needs of all your students.

Scaffolding

On more cognitively complex tasks, sometimes one student gets stuck and sometimes entire groups get stuck. If a group gets stuck, here are three quick scaffolds to keep students and groups moving:

- One stray, three stay: One student goes on a reconnaissance mission to see what other groups are thinking. This should be a quick trip and then back to work.

- Two stray, one stay: This approach may be more helpful if you have a group that is really stuck or you know that multiple students in the group can benefit from hearing outside perspectives.

- Give one, get one: This approach helps if the entire class is stuck. All students find a student outside their group, give one hint, get one hint, and then go back to their group and share what they learned.

Extending

Here are some ways to extend structured grouping:

- Give accelerated students the more difficult roles to play in a group.

- Ask students to share and defend multiple perspectives or perspectives different than their own.

- Ask students to make generalizations based on the multiple perspectives they have heard within their structured groups.

Instructional Technique 5

COOPERATIVE PROJECTS

There are two differences between this technique and the previous one, structured grouping. Structured grouping is best suited for short-term projects that serve to deepen students' knowledge during the ongoing progression of an instructional unit. Cooperative projects, on the other hand, last longer and are usually assigned at the end of a learning progression to give students opportunities to apply or use their knowledge.

Cooperative projects should include structured positive interdependence and individual accountability. Groups for long-term projects can be a source of frustration for students if this technique is not thoughtfully designed and monitored. Students need to know what individual expectations are for the end work product they will submit. This technique describes options for dividing the project into parts that they complete cooperatively and parts that they complete individually. For example, students might work together to gather, share, and organize information, but execute all of the other components of the project individually. This split approach gives students the benefit of hearing multiple perspectives as they learn as well as holds them individually accountable for demonstrating their learning.

How to Effectively Implement Cooperative Projects

As with other techniques in this guide, planning for cooperative projects has multiple aspects to consider. As you read through each section that follows, think about how you will implement cooperative projects in your own classroom.

Identify Critical Content

The first step is to identify critical content. Because cooperative projects take time, make sure that the critical content is cognitively complex. If your students spend too much time on critical content that is not cognitively complex, you may never find time to reach the rigor of standards. When students are assigned to participate in projects that require higher-order thinking, they are more likely to have success in their interactions with each other. Open-ended questions that require complex thinking allow students to share perspectives and debate one another. If the project poses questions that have only one correct answer, you will more likely find students copying from their peers or dividing the work load since no real reason exists to discuss and examine their thinking with each other.

Plan a Meaningful Task

Create a task that requires students to either want or need to work together. Give students a substantial reason for working in a group or they will choose to work alone. Students must understand and come to strongly believe that they are more effective and can accomplish more with the help of their group members. At the same time, if students know they will be accountable for the demonstration of their own learning, they will be unable to ride on the coattails of their peers.

Some suggestions for how to blend individual and group accountability within projects include:

- individual explanations in which students create the work product cooperatively, and then each student explains it individually

- component parts in which the entire task is broken into sections or parts, each demonstrating the learning target(s), and then assembled into the finished product

- separate tasks in which students learn the concepts within their groups but are given individual tasks to evaluate their performance

- individual performance in which each student in the group completes the entire task and then explains or presents it to their small groups, which then discuss the content

- individual products in which students who are completing the same type of task collaborate, but all students create their own products

If you choose the last option in the previous set of suggestions—individual products with group collaboration—think about how to incorporate flexible grouping, in which students collaborate with each other for parts and work alone or with different groups for other parts. This can be advantageous because students get collaboration opportunities to learn from and bounce ideas off their peers, but they also have individual accountability. Any part of a long-term project can become a collaborative learning opportunity. Here is a list of ways for students to collaborate during a long-term project:

- brainstorm hypotheses

- gather and share information

- discuss options for organizing the information

- discuss the strengths of supporting documentation for their claims

- generate conclusions

If students work together for a significant portion of a cooperative project, think about how to make them individually accountable for their own participation in the project. One option is to expect students to keep reflective journals in which they make regular entries about their work devoted to the group goal. Teachers or peers should review these entries and give feedback throughout the process. A second option is a group reflection sheet in which students reflect about group dynamics and progress so the teacher can help adjust for issues that arise.

Structure Intentional Interactions

Plan ahead of time how students will interact during cooperative projects. Group interactions must be an exchange of ideas, not simply an opportunity for students to divide up the tasks in the project. The conversations should be centered on the essential knowledge and skills of the learning target and help students analyze their thinking. Provide guidance for what these conversations sound like since students may not be used to exchanging academic ideas with their peers. Discuss the differences between collaboration and cheating. Many students are not certain where they should draw the line, because they have had few opportunities to collaborate.

Chunk the project into manageable parts. Make plans for when, with whom, and how students will interact with each other. Set a timeline for the interactions throughout the project, and specifically describe a desired outcome for those interactions. Maintain the timelines, being flexible when necessary. When the cooperative project is first explained, allow time for:

- brainstorming of possible ways to demonstrate the learning targets

- identification of individual responsibilities of each group member

- agreement upon meeting time if the assignment is not completed in class

Have students create a checklist of responsibilities that are individual and responsibilities that they share. Within their groups, have students agree on who will ensure each shared responsibility is completed. Help students set deadlines for each of the responsibilities. This will help you and the students know whether they are on track throughout the project.

Organize Students Into Groups

If you are using flexible grouping for the student interactions during the project, you might let students select their own group based on particular needs. When letting students select their groups, give them guidelines to follow and suggestions as to how and why they should select a specific group. For instance, students might join a group with other students who have the same hypothesis to brainstorm where to find resources to support their claim. Students might meet with other students who are using the same medium; for example, an essay or PowerPoint to convey their responses. If you allow students to pick their own groups without giving them any selection criteria, they will most often pick their friends. Provide various topic options and then let students vote with their feet and join a group.

If students are presenting their projects, think about dividing the class into smaller groups for the presentations. Have each student present to a small group while you walk around listening. If the presentation is electronic, borrow another projector and divide the class into two or more groups of listeners so that students present simultaneously. Unless you are assessing a speaking standard, you do not need to be fully engaged in every presentation. Just ensure that you have documentation to later assess the work product.

If you do decide on a whole-class share out, require students to actively engage during presentations. Students should not only take notes but also use higher-order thinking skills by responding in writing to what they are hearing. Have them compare their responses with other students or ask them to synthesize the information from the presentation to generate a conclusion.

Establish Routines

Projects can become derailed without routines, and cooperative projects are no exception. Provide timelines and check-in points. This is especially key if you are asking students to work in groups for long periods of time. Do not hesitate to tell students that the class is moving on and they will need to catch up. Some students will use as much time as you provide, and they will not always use it wisely, so set a time limit, and stick to it. That does not mean you will not accept any work after the time is done, it means you explain and expect them to work on the next part of the project in the timeline so they will need to accelerate their pace or catch up at home.

If students are working independently for the majority of the project, you may want them to interact with each other for specific reasons within the timeline. Do not be afraid to restrict students to a brief period of time (five to ten minutes) to work together before working alone again. Sometimes setting time limits may mean that students who do not use their time wisely miss out on the opportunity to collaborate. This consequence may help them avoid that mistake in the future.

Teach and Reinforce Conative Skills

When students work together for extended periods of time, controversy and conflict are bound to arise. Because controversy and conflict have different root causes, you should handle them differently in the classroom.

Controversy occurs when two people with incompatible beliefs disagree (Marzano, 2013). This can occur quite often in a class where students interact with each other to discuss ideas. The problem is not the disagreement, but how they handle the disagreement. Your role is to help students interact productively so they can learn from each other. Controversy can be beneficial because it usually leads to better ideas and deeper thinking. Therefore, directly teach students how to handle controversy when it arises.

Create a protocol for students to follow that prompts them to share their perspectives and reasoning, listen to their partners' perspectives and reasoning, and then reach an agreement.

A possible protocol could be:

1. Student A shares her perspective and reasoning, citing evidence when necessary.

2. Student B summarizes what he heard and asks for clarification as necessary.

3. Student B shares his perspective and reasoning, citing evidence when necessary.

4. Student A summarizes what she heard and asks for clarification as necessary.

5. Students brainstorm other possible perspectives.

6. Students work together to come to an agreement, citing evidence for the agreement.

In younger grades, the protocol could be written as:

1. Student A: What do you think and why?

2. Student B: What did Student A say?

3. Student B: What do you think and why?

4. Student A: What did Student B say?

5. Both students: What are some other ideas that might help?

6. Both students: What can you both agree on?

Conflict occurs when one person is getting in the way of another's goals (Marzano, 2013). Conflict is different than controversy because it is usually not productive; it will not result in better ideas. It can often interfere with learning. Conflict may arise when students interact with each other. Two students may want to use the same resource at the same time. One student may feel that another student talks too much or does not work hard enough. Partners may not be able to agree on an idea for the project. When supporting students as they handle conflict, help them focus on the problem rather than the individual with whom they disagree. The most effective way to resolve conflicts is through a problem-solving negotiation. The following protocol is adapted from Johnson & Johnson (2005) and Marzano (2013):

1. State the goal: Students state what they want.

2. State feelings: Students state how they feel about the situation.

3. State reasons for wants and feelings: Students explain why they feel the way they do.

4. Reverse perspectives: Students state the perspectives of others.

5. Create potential agreements: Students identify a variety of possible agreements.

6. Settle: Students settle on one of the agreements.

Common Mistakes

There are several ways that your implementation of cooperative projects can go wrong. Consider the following common mistakes and plan ahead to avoid them:

- The teacher does not assign a task that requires students to share ideas and perspectives to complete the task.

- The teacher allows students to divide the project and work independently.

- The teacher does not check in with student groups throughout the project.

- The teacher does not ensure that student interaction is meaningfully centered on the project.

- The teacher does not require individual accountability.

- The teacher expects students to handle controversy and conflicts themselves without teacher intervention and support.

Examples and Nonexamples of Grouping for Cooperative Projects

The following examples and nonexamples have been provided to help you better understand how to implement this technique in your classroom. While the example may not feature the same grade or subject you teach, look for the commonalties between your class and the examples so that you can begin to imagine how you can implement this technique with your students.

Elementary Example of Cooperative Projects

The learning target students will demonstrate for this cooperative project is: *on a map of North America, identify the first 13 colonies and describe how regional differences in climate, types of farming, populations and sources of labor shaped their economies throughout the 18th century* (Massachusetts History and Social Science Curriculum Framework 5th grade 5.10). Students have already identified the thirteen colonies and the three regions. The teacher makes multiple resources available for students to use and provides them with a graphic organizer to record their thinking as they collect the information.

> For the next few days during social studies class, we will work on our project. Every day you will have a section to complete. Each student in a group of three will identify the following for their region of the colonies: climate, types of farming, populations, sources of labor, and economy. Today, I want you to decide among your group mates who will research which region. I also want you to identify the climate and the populations for your region. That will take a chunk of time, so please don't get distracted looking up other information about your region.

The teacher then highlights some of the available resources and makes sure all students have a graphic organizer. As students start to organize themselves and research their regions, the teacher facilitates conversations about where to find information about climate and population. Before the end of class, the teacher asks the students to report their findings to their group members and take notes on the information their group members collected.

The teacher continues the project the next day by asking students to research types of farming and sources of labor. During the third class period, the students research and share the economies for their regions, and the teacher holds a class discussion about how some of the factors may have influenced the economy of each region.

At the start of the fourth class period, the teacher reviews the factors: climate, types of farming, populations, sources of labor, and economy. She then directs students to their groups to discuss and record how they each think these factors influence the economies of the three regions.

During the fifth class period, the teacher asks students to work individually using their graphic organizers to record the factors that shaped the economy for each region. Each student identifies the factors and their influence on the economy of each of the three regions on a map.

Elementary Nonexample of Cooperative Projects

In the nonexample classroom, the students use the graphic organizer to take notes on each of the factors as the teacher explains them. The students are then given one map per group of three students and the teacher asks them to identify the factors and their influence on the economy of each of the three regions. Because the students have not been given individual responsibilities or task, the teacher cannot identify which students are able to demonstrate the learning target.

Secondary Example of Cooperative Projects

In this example, the high school life science teacher creates a project for students to complete together to demonstrate the following learning target: *design, evaluate, and refine a solution for reducing the impacts of human activities on the environment and biodiversity* (NGSS High School Life Science HS-LS2-7). The project focuses on a hypothetical dam being built on a nearby river. To aid in understanding the impacts of the dam, the teacher adds the hypothetical dam to a topographical map of the area for students to use. This cooperative project has five steps:

1. With your group: Identify the potential impacts of the dam on the environment and biodiversity in the area.

2. With your group: Brainstorm characteristics of a solution to reduce the impacts of the dam on the environment and biodiversity in the area.

3. Individually: Design your solution for reducing the impacts.

4. With your group: Evaluate each other's designs based on the characteristics previously identified.

5. Individually: Refine your design based on feedback.

The students have worked together often in the past, so the teacher does not spend much time on the routines of how to effectively interact with each other. However, she does set specific time limits for each of the five steps of this project and requires proof of completion of the step at the designated time. As the students work in their groups, the teacher moves efficiently among them, helping students stay focused on the topic and effectively handles any conflicts or controversies that arise. She directs groups that get stuck to listen in on other conversations to get unstuck and points them to specific resources that are available. Students turn in their original and revised designs as proof that they were able to demonstrate the learning target.

Secondary Nonexample of Cooperative Projects

In this nonexample, the class is focused on the same learning target: *design, evaluate, and refine a solution for reducing the impacts of human activities on the environment and biodiversity* (NGSS High School Life Science HS-LS2-7). The teacher is worried that the groups will not be able to identify the potential impacts or correct characteristics of potential solutions, so instead of facilitating group work, she makes it a point to go to every group to lead a discussion on those two topics. Students quickly realize that if they write down her explanations they will be correct, so there is little discussion between students. In this nonexample, the teacher does the majority of the talking.

Determining If Students Work Cooperatively to Complete Projects

The only way to know if students are working cooperatively to complete projects is to witness evidence of it throughout the various steps of the project. If you wait until students turn in their final project, you will be too late to intervene and redirect. Here are some ways you can monitor that students are working cooperatively to complete a project:

- Ask students to describe their individual contribution to the group on a card, and collect the cards to verify the accuracy.

- Look over the responsibility checklist to ensure that all students are contributing.

- Listen as groups interact to check that students are sharing their own perspectives.

- Look over partial projects from each student to determine if they are focusing on the critical content.

- Ask students to rate their peers from one to five for contribution to the group and justify their ratings. Collect and review the ratings to target students who need extra support to contribute equally.

Table 5.1 is a student proficiency scale for cooperative projects that you can use and adapt as necessary to determine how students are progressing in their abilities to work cooperatively during long-term group projects.

Table 5.1: Student Proficiency Scale for Cooperative Projects

Emerging	Fundamental	Desired Result
Students talk about content.	Students actively participate.	Students interact responsibly and equally.
Students listen as other students talk about content.	Students listen to others and discuss their own understanding of the critical content.	Students demonstrate mastery of the critical content.
Students know the group's responsibilities for the project.	Students know individual and shared responsibilities for the project.	Students can explain how their understanding and the understanding of their group mates are similar and different. Students can explain how they and their group mates contributed to the project.

Scaffold and Extend Instruction to Meet Students' Needs

This technique has focused on many aspects to consider when implementing cooperative projects, but only you know the needs of your individual students. Intentionally plan how you will scaffold or extend instruction to meet the needs of all your students.

Scaffolding

Think ahead of time how you will support students who might struggle with cooperative projects. Identify what you think their particular problems will be and plan for adaptations you can use as needed.

- Create job cards that describe the students' responsibilities in the group.

- Provide a detailed timeline of individual and shared responsibilities.

- Prepare a list of questions that might spark discussion.

Extending

Some students come to your classroom more prepared for group interaction and individual accountability than others. If students are advanced, we still need to raise our expectations for them.

- Ask students to brainstorm a list of responsibilities and timeline for completion.

- Let students decide when and how to work with their peers and when to work alone.

- Ask students to describe how their strengths helped them contribute and how they could be more effective next time.

Instructional Technique 6

PEER RESPONSE GROUPS

You can periodically conduct formal peer response groups to allow students to share drafts of their work in progress or elicit peer feedback and coaching advice on maintaining strengths and eliminating possible weaknesses (Marzano & Brown, 2009). Projects and other complex tasks that are completed individually can benefit from group interactions through peer response groups. Structuring timely, specific feedback within the context of the learning process helps students clarify the learning target, therefore resulting in a higher quality product. Timely peer feedback also facilitates perspective sharing so that students have opportunities to hear other students' perspectives to help them deepen their understanding of critical content.

Peer response groups can be a helpful source of feedback for students. Both the individual who is giving feedback and the individual who is receiving it benefit from another perspective. Before you read about how to implement peer response groups, note the benefits and potential obstacles so that you can plan for the most effective groups possible.

Benefits
- Encourage students to analyze work.
- Help clarify assessment criteria.
- Give students a wider range of feedback.
- Closely parallel possible career situations.

Potential Obstacles
- Students may lack ability to provide accurate feedback.
- Students may not take giving feedback seriously.
- Students may feel discriminated against or misunderstood.
- Students may misinform each other.

Structure and guidance can lessen or overcome the potential obstacles.

How to Effectively Implement Peer Response Groups

The effective implementation of peer response groups uses the same steps in the other techniques. As you read, note how you can apply this technique in your own classroom.

Identify Critical Content

Identify a specific piece of work in which students have been required to demonstrate their understanding and communication of complex thinking. If the work product only requires yes/no or right/wrong responses, there would be no need for detailed peer feedback. In these cases, there are no perspectives for students to share. Peer response groups work well with long-term projects and other more cognitively complex work in which students examine their reasoning by stating and supporting a claim or examine similarities and differences between aspects of critical content.

Plan a Meaningful Task

Peer feedback needs to occur within the allocated work time. Let students know in advance that before they turn in their assignments, you expect them to solicit peer feedback and revise their work accordingly. To realize the benefits of peer response groups to the fullest extent possible, ensure that the groups are focused on work products that are closely aligned to a learning target. Without guidance, students will often provide feedback similar to the types they have received in prior grades or classes. For example, they will correct spelling mistakes and point out grammatical issues. However, unless spelling and grammar are part of the learning target, they should not be the focus of the feedback given in peer response groups. When you pair students for feedback, give them specific questions to answer. Students should not make value judgments. Effective feedback answers three questions:

> Feed up: Where am I going? Provide feedback on how well the student demonstrated the learning target.

> Feedback: How am I going? Give the student feedback on the process he is using.

> Feed forward: Where to next? Provide suggestions for growth. (Adapted from Hattie, 2008.)

When you create the specific questions for students, keep these types of feedback in mind. Students can identify strengths, state whether they were able to find the information they looked for, or determine whether they met the learning target. Students can also react to the feedback by stating what they understood or what might have been confusing. Please note that student feedback should never replace teacher monitoring and assessment of student learning.

Here are some sentence stems to use for peer response groups:

Feed up:

- I highlighted that part of the learning target because . . .

- You demonstrated the learning target when you . . .

Feedback:

- It was effective when you _____ because . . .

- I like that you . . . because . . .

- I was not sure why you . . .

- An interesting part of your response was _____ because . . .

Feed forward:

- To move up on the scale, you could work on . . .

- The area that could be improved is _____ because . . .

When you first implement this technique with your students, use a sample work product and model for them how to answer the questions and provide feedback. You can create a sample yourself, use one from a previous year, or ask a student privately if he will let you use his work to model the process. Asking a student to use his work is effective if you choose a resilient student that you expect has created a solid, but not perfect, piece of work. Make sure to model what you expect to see and hear, and be truthful, positive, and specific in your feedback. To model peer feedback, here are some possible steps. Adapt them to meet the specific context of your lesson.

Modeling peer feedback:

- Hand out copies of a sample work.

- Discuss the guiding questions that will be answered.

- Discuss the critical content about which to give feedback.

- Read the sample work and think aloud about the strengths of the work.

- Demonstrate how you would answer the guiding questions by thinking out loud as you provide feedback.

- Ask students to read the work and add to your responses.

- Discuss the responses as a class.

Help students focus on giving specific, actionable responses by providing guidelines for the quality of feedback, such as the following:

- Read the work all the way through before you comment.

- Point out the strengths of the work.

- Offer polite, appropriate, constructive comments from a reader's point of view.

- Make comments work-specific, and stick to the critical content.

- Before giving your written comments to a group member, reread your comments to make sure they are clear and understandable.

A variation of this technique is to have students compare responses rather than critique each other's responses. Students compare their answers and describe what is similar and different but do not critique each other's work. Comparing answers can help when students first begin interacting with each other in peer response groups. Students have opportunities to listen to other responses without feeling criticized for their own work.

Structure Intentional Interactions

Students need clearly stated expectations that they will both present their feedback and listen to feedback from others. This should be a structured experience that does not deteriorate into highly charged arguments regarding the value and accuracy of the feedback.

There are five steps for intentional interaction in peer response groups:

1. Students read over each other's work.

2. Students answer specific questions to provide feedback on each other's work.

3. Students state what they learned from reading the other person's work.

4. Students state what they learned as a result of the feedback.

5. Students revise their own work.

You may want to write each step on the board and set a timer so that students know when to move from one step to the next.

Organize Students Into Groups

Quite often homogenous grouping works best for student response groups; students can get feedback from someone with similar academic success. A struggling student may have a difficult time giving useful feedback to a student whose work is academically sophisticated. When deciding how to group, think about the depth of responses that students have provided this far in the current unit, since students may differ in their strengths from unit to unit. Also consider any other academic strengths students may have. You might pair two strong writers, two students who describe details well, or two students who struggle with sentence structure. Organizing your students into groups is an opportunity to push your students to greater academic rigor, so pair wisely.

Establish Routines

Before your students begin any work, let them know when they will work in their peer response groups and the topic or project about which they will provide feedback. Be consistent in your use of routines. If students do not have enough work completed to receive authentic feedback, do not partner them with someone who does. Instead, partner them with someone else who is also not done, and provide that group with a copy of another student's completed work. Ask them to provide feedback on this work, similar to how you modeled feedback.

Teach and Reinforce Conative Skills

Do not ask students to provide and receive feedback if they do not believe they are able to improve. Individuals can often mistakenly believe that abilities such as creativity, artistic ability, and athleticism are fixed and that those abilities cannot be changed. However, abilities, including intelligence, can be cultivated. People with a growth mindset believe they can increase their intelligence along with other abilities. A growth mindset is necessary for students to persevere when they do not succeed the first time they try something. The good news is that you can motivate and cultivate growth mindsets in your students.

To cultivate growth mindsets, help your students to become more aware of when they exhibit fixed mindsets with statements such as, "I'm not good at math." Help them understand that just because they may have struggled with a subject or content in the past does not mean they are not capable of learning. Praise their efforts rather than their intelligence. Affirm their efforts and point out specific projects or skills where they have shown creativity or deeper thinking. Discuss other people who have overcome obstacles with hard work and determination.

Common Mistakes

While feedback from peers is the essence of this technique, feedback from peers should not replace feedback from the teacher. For peer response groups to be productive and useful to students, here are some common mistakes to avoid along the way:

- The teacher asks students to provide feedback too frequently or on too much critical content.

- The teacher does not tell students to expect peer feedback, so they are caught by surprise when told that peers will see their work.

- The teacher waits until the due date to incorporate peer response groups, not giving students adequate time to revise their work after feedback.

- The teacher asks students to grade the work for the teacher.

- The teacher does not have students go back and revise their work products based on the feedback they received.

- The teacher does not specify what type of feedback to give.

Examples and Nonexamples of Grouping for Peer Response Groups

As you read these two examples and their corresponding nonexamples, think about how these teachers skillfully avoid or make one of the common mistakes discussed.

Elementary Example of Peer Response Groups

The learning target for this elementary example is: *use adjectives and adverbs, and choose between them depending on what is to be modified* (CCSS Language K-5, 2nd grade). The example teacher has chosen to isolate this skill to allow students to give feedback to each other as they create sentences. The class is learning about deserts in science, so she decides to combine the practice of the targeted skill with the information students have learned about deserts. To prepare for this activity, the teacher has assigned student partners and given each student a mini-whiteboard to write on. She begins her lesson:

> Class, remember what we previously learned about adjectives and adverbs. Adjectives describe nouns, and adverbs describe verbs. Today, we will practice using adjectives and adverbs in our writing about deserts. Here are some pictures of deserts to help you remember what you learned in science. I want you to write one sentence about deserts. Make sure that sentence has both an adjective and an adverb in it.

The teacher walks around, directing students to use the word wall as a resource if they cannot think of an adjective or adverb for their sentences. When the students have completed their sentences, the teacher continues.

> Now I want you to read over your partner's sentence. Please circle the adjective and underline the adverb. Put a triangle around the noun if the adjective is missing and a triangle around the verb if the adverb is missing. Next, I want you to tell your partner, "I like that you . . ." Or ask the question, "How could you describe . . . ?" I've written those sentence starters on the board for you to use.

As the students talk to their partners, the teacher walks around, checking to see whether students have triangles on their whiteboards and listening to partners to ensure they are providing feedback specific to adjectives and adverbs.

> Class, now that you have received feedback on your sentence, work on it again. Even if you had an adjective and an adverb in your sentence, change them. Can you be more specific? Can you be more imaginative?

The students then revise their sentences based on feedback. The lesson continues with students writing another sentence without feedback from their partners to practice independently.

Elementary Nonexample of Peer Response Groups

The nonexample teacher sets up the same lesson and has students write their sentences. Then, instead of having students circle and underline the nouns, verbs, adjectives, and adverbs, she simply instructs them to "help your partner make a better sentence." Without clear direction regarding how to give effective feedback, some students end up rewriting sentences for students who need assistance rather than giving them pointers and asking them questions.

Secondary Example of Peer Response Groups

The learning target in this art class is: *identify, select, and use elements and principles to organize the composition in his or her own artwork* (Arizona

Visual Arts Standard PO 201). The students will receive feedback from peers on their use of perspective in their drawings during this lesson. For all students to receive feedback that is appropriate for growth, the teacher has partnered students according to their abilities to demonstrate perspective so that students who have grasped the concept are giving feedback to other students who have grasped the concept. He has the following three feedback sentence starters on the board.

- You demonstrated effective perspective by . . .

- An interesting part of your drawing is _____ because . . .

- The part of your drawing that you could work on is _____ because . . .

The teacher also has one self-reflection sentence starter on the board:

- I will improve perspective in my drawing by . . .

> When you are giving feedback to your peers, don't tell them everything they need to improve. Simply respond to the first three questions on the board. Please take some time to study your partner's drawing and answer those questions in writing. I will tell you when it's time to begin sharing with your partner.

As students are silently looking and writing, the teacher walks around to check that the feedback is staying focused on perspective. After a few minutes, the teacher lets the groups that are done writing begin to share with each other until all groups are discussing their responses. While groups are discussing, the teacher walks around to ensure that no conversations become heated and that feedback is given and received in the manner it is intended— for growth. When students finish giving and receiving feedback, the teacher directs them to answer the fourth question on the board. Based on this feedback, "I will improve perspective in my drawing by . . ." students then return to quietly working on their drawings, improving them based on the feedback they received.

Secondary Nonexample of Peer Response Groups

In this nonexample, the teacher leads the class through all the same steps as the example teacher with one exception. He posts only the first three questions and does not explicitly ask students to use the feedback they received to improve their work. Without follow-through, some students do not apply what they learned from their peer response groups to make revisions to enhance their work, missing an opportunity to deepen their understanding of using perspective in their drawings.

Determining If Students Can Effectively Interact in Peer Response Groups

To determine if peer response grouping has achieved the desired result, verify that your students effectively interact and learn as they provide and receive feedback in peer response groups.

For this to occur, two things have to happen:

1. Your students need to actively participate in a small-group discussion about the strengths and opportunities for growth in their work and revise their work as a result.

2. You, the teacher, must engage in some kind of monitoring action to listen, look for, read, check, inspect, or otherwise determine that your students are doing this.

This two-step process ensures that your students are exhibiting the desired result, and that you are aware of it. Consider the following suggestions for how to monitor for the desired result of peer response groups.

- As students are writing down their feedback, read over their shoulders to ensure they focus on critical content.

- Have students summarize their discussions and then read through the summaries.

- Ask students to reflect on what they learned from the discussion on their original work so that you can read it when they submit their final work.

- Listen as students discuss their feedback, so you can ensure it is accurate and actionable.

- Ask students to write about an area of growth on their whiteboards and hold it up so you can scan them for relevance to the critical content.

Use the student proficiency scale for peer response groups found in Table 6.1 to determine how effectively your students are interacting and learning as they provide and receive feedback from each other.

Table 6.1: Student Proficiency Scale for Peer Response Groups

Emerging	Fundamental	Desired Result
Students provide feedback.	Students provide accurate, actionable feedback.	Students provide accurate, specific feedback about the learning target, the process used in their partners' work, and suggestions for growth.
Students discuss both partners' work.	Students state strengths and opportunities for growth in their partners' work.	Students actively participate in a discussion about the strengths and opportunities for growth in both partners' work.
Students make some revisions to their work.	Students revise their work after the interaction.	Students use what they learned in the group interaction to enhance their work.

Scaffold and Extend Instruction to Meet Students' Needs

Adapting techniques is sometimes necessary to meet the needs of students and does not have to be complicated. Adaptations can be small, as long as they help students grow, effectively interact, and learn as they provide and receive feedback from each other.

Scaffolding

You will likely encounter some students who need extra support as they provide feedback in peer response groups.

- Ask students to focus on one specific aspect or piece of critical content rather than the work as a whole. This will help students give and receive feedback without being overwhelmed by all that might be improved.

- Have examples and nonexamples of effective feedback available for students to refer to, so if they are not sure how to finish a sentence starter, they can seek out examples of effective feedback.

Extending

Groups of students that demonstrate the learning target prior to receiving feedback need to enhance and deepen their work product in more complex ways.

- Have groups of students give and receive feedback regarding how to add more detail to one's work or how to cite more evidence regarding a claim.

- Have students revise a piece of work that is not their own to demonstrate the learning target in a different way.

Instructional Technique 7

GROUP REFLECTING ON LEARNING

Within the instructional sequence, students need to take time to reflect on what they are learning. This technique involves students working in groups to reflect on different aspects of learning. Students can reflect independently, but like many other aspects of learning, student interaction enhances reflection. Reflecting in a group setting allows students to hear other perspectives, learn from others' mistakes, and celebrate the successes of others. Discussion in small groups allows students to express their feelings about learning in a safe setting. Students are more likely to say, "I don't understand," in a small peer group than they may be during a whole-class discussion. Due to the power dynamic between teachers and students, students often find it too risky to open up about their struggles and confusion to a teacher, whereas they may be more willing to have those conversations with peers. This technique allows students to provide support for each other in their journeys toward demonstrating mastery of the standards. When students reflect together, they realize they are not alone in the learning journey. They can find comfort in the struggles and triumphs of others.

How to Effectively Implement Group Reflecting on Learning

Similarly to previous techniques, there are six teacher behaviors to effectively implement group reflecting on learning: 1) identifying critical content, 2) planning a meaningful task, 3) structuring intentional interaction, 4) organizing students into groups, 5) establishing routines for interacting, and 6) teaching and reinforcing conative skills.

Identify Critical Content

The critical content of this strategy differs from the critical content in previous techniques. To effectively implement group reflecting on learning, guide your students to reflect on one of three things: 1) their progress toward achieving a learning target or goal, 2) any one of a number of processes in which they have engaged with peers during learning, or 3) a work product they have created.

Reflect on Progress

The first way students can reflect on learning is to examine and evaluate their progress toward achieving a specific academic goal. For students to reflect on their progress, you must consistently share learning goals and targets with students as well as explain any applicable performance or proficiency scales before learning begins.

Reflect on the Process

Secondly, students can reflect on how they are learning. To do this, you might ask them to focus on how well they interacted with each other, how satisfied they are with the quality and amount of their participation in class, and what strengths they believe they brought to their group effort.

Reflect on the Product

Finally, students can reflect on the outcome of their learning. These outcomes might consist of a section of a project, entries in their academic notebooks, or written responses on which they have received feedback from peers and the teacher. Students can reflect on what they did well and what they learned through producing those products.

Plan a Meaningful Task

In this metacognitive technique, students have opportunities to discuss their reflections on learning with peers. They are encouraged and expected to think about and discuss aspects of learning in ways that most students may not do on their own. To facilitate this type of reflection about learning, develop reflection questions specifically for the type of reflection you want students to focus on.

Progress:

- Did you and your partner demonstrate the learning target? What is your next step in learning?

- Where are you on the performance scale? Where is your partner? What can you and your partner do to help move each other forward?

Process:

- What strengths did you and your group members bring to the conversation today?

- How did each of you contribute to the group today?

- What would you do differently as a group to learn more the next time you work together?

Product:

- Compare your responses with your partner. How does your work product differ from your partner's product? For what aspects of the task did you respond similarly to your partner?

- What feedback did your partner receive that can help you?

Provide a reflection form for students if you feel they need more direction than these open-ended questions will provide. Figure 7.1 is an example of an organizer to help elementary students reflect on how well they worked with their partner during a lesson.

Figure 7.1: Reflective Organizer for Elementary Students

Today my partner and I chose to _____.

I felt:

☺   ☹   **?**

Happy   Sad   Confused

Next time we will _____.

Figure 7.2 is an example of a graphic organizer to help middle or high school students discuss their contributions to group work.

Figure 7.2: Graphic Organizer for Reflection at the Secondary Level

I contributed to the group by . . .
This helped the group because . . .
Next time I do group work, I will . . .

Structure Intentional Interactions

Throughout instruction, direct students to intentionally stop and reflect on their learning. Student interaction for this technique is similar to the previous techniques in that students must first gather their thoughts privately before they are ready share their own perspectives and listen to their partners' reflections as part of their intentional interaction. Here are the steps to this intentional interaction process:

1. Students reflect on their learning.

2. Students share their reflections.

3. Students provide specific statements of encouragement and support to their partners.

4. Students state what their next steps are for growth based on their partners' feedback.

If there are more than two students in the group, they can also implement this technique as a round robin, in which students go around the circle to share, encourage, and support the person to their left (or right).

Organize Students Into Groups

This technique lends itself well to ad hoc grouping in which student groups are formed only for this technique. Groups of two work well because students are often reluctant to reflect on how much they have learned in a larger group; but, once your students become used to metacognitive conversation, you can create larger groups so your students can hear multiple perspectives.

You might also consider using informal, unplanned grouping for this technique. To allow students to choose their partners with little planning on your part, consider some of the following:

- When you want students to find a partner, establish a routine to play music. While the music is playing, students walk around the room. When the music stops, the closest students partner together.

- Use the compass partners exercise in which students find four different partners (north, south, east, west) to pair with throughout the lesson or during the week (see Figure 7.3 for a compass partners form).

- Use speed dial partners, in which students sign up to be a specific number on each other's speed dial. Then for each discussion question, they move to the next partner on their list. This allows any number of pairings (see Figure 7.4 for a speed dial partners form).

- Use an electronic app or program that randomly groups students for you.

- Pass out one playing card to each student. The students with cards of the same value partner up.

Figure 7.3 is an example of a compass partners form for students to use in forming partner groups. Before the lesson starts, ask students to find four partners. Each partner signs the other partner's card at the appropriate compass point. It is important that they both sign at the same compass point. For each pairing, call out a compass point and ask students to meet with the person whose name is written at that compass point.

Figure 7.3: Compass Partners Form

North Partner

_____

West Partner   **East Partner**

_____   _____

South Partner

_____

Figure 7.4 is an example of a speed dial partners form to use in helping students form reflective groups.

Figure 7.4: Speed Dial Partners Form

1:
2:
3:
4:
5:
6:

Establish Routines

No matter how you choose to organize your students, take the time to establish routines for students to partner that are quick and efficient. Designate which partner will speak first. Use something random, such as which partner is closest to the door, which partner has the longest response, or which partner went last, if the students have been paired previously. A little bit of structure can help facilitate a successful group interaction. If you have a group of three due to an odd number of students in your class, remind them that they will have less time per student than other groups, so they will need to talk quickly.

Teach and Reinforce Conative Skills

When students are asked to reflect on their learning, they may reflexively engage in negative thinking without realizing it. Negative thinking can be categorized as emotional thinking and worrying. Emotional thinking is when someone allows emotions to dictate their thoughts and actions. When it appears that students are struggling with this, help them understand that their emotions do not need to dictate their actions. Even if they are not confident in their learning, they should not stop trying. A poor grade on a single test does not mean they are unable to learn. When students are reflecting on their learning, help them disconnect their emotions from their actions so they do not give up and quit trying. Worrying involves persistent negative thoughts. Students who have not experienced academic success may often think negatively about their performance, even when evidence suggests otherwise. You can assist these students by helping them become aware of how often they worry. Help them monitor their inner dialogue, and give them positive statements to say when they find themselves worrying. As they discuss their learning with their partners, help reframe their statements by modeling less negative thinking for them.

Common Mistakes

Mistakes open the door for learning. Here is a list of common mistakes you can learn from as you plan to implement this technique:

- The teacher does not have routines for how to partner students or structure interactions.

- The teacher asks content questions rather than reflection questions.

- The teacher does not connect the reflection activity to the learning target.

- The teacher changes the partnering routine so often that students waste class time learning new partnering techniques.

- The teacher does not hold students accountable for their reflections, allowing some students to consistently avoid reflecting on their learning.

Examples and Nonexamples of Group Reflecting on Learning

Following are two examples (one elementary and one secondary) and their corresponding nonexamples illustrating how students can work in groups to reflect on their learning. As you read them, think about your own classroom and how you can make this technique come to life for your students.

Elementary Example of Group Reflecting on Learning

This example can be used in any elementary class at the end of any lesson.

The students have just finished an activity, and there is not much time left in class when the music begins. Students immediately recognize the signal, so they stand up and start moving around the room. When the music stops, they find the person nearest to them and face them. The teacher watches and quickly helps unpartnered students find each other. Realizing there is an odd number of students that day, she asks a group of two to invite the remaining student into their group.

> I want you to take a moment to reflect on what you learned today. We've already talked about the performance scale on the board a few times, so I want you to think silently about where you would put yourself on the scale and why. First, think about what you did in class today related to the scale. Were you successful in doing it by yourself, or did you need help from one of your group members or me? If you needed help, that's OK, but then you can't say you are that level of the scale. Remember that level of the scale means you can do it by yourself. So if you got help with something today, look at the level of the scale below that to see if you can do those things by yourself. Once you've silently decided what level of the scale you are on and can explain why, give me a thumbs-up.

As the students do this, the teacher walks around in case students want to have a quiet conversation with her. When she has seen a thumbs-up from the students, she continues.

> Now I want each of you to tell your partner where on the performance scale you rated yourself and how you know you have attained that rating. Partners, if the answer does not make sense to you, ask questions. Push your partner politely to be truthful. Do not tell your partners where you think they are on the scale; ask them to explain their answer. If your partner has moved up the scale because she learned something today, give her a silent high five or tell her congratulations. Let's celebrate our learning! I will set the timer so you each have one minute to talk, and I want the tallest person in the pair to go first.

As the students talk, the teacher walks around listening to the responses and helping students correctly identify where they are on the scale. She also stops to celebrate with pairs in which students have moved up the scale.

Elementary Nonexample of Group Reflecting on Learning

The nonexample teacher decides to try the activity since it works so well for the teacher down the hall. The students are not used to the routine of using music to get in groups. Nor are they in the habit of reflecting on their learning. The teacher takes the time to explain how to get in groups when the music stops and also explains each level of the scale. This process delays the end of the lesson, and the students start to get impatient because the teacher is cutting into recess time. Realizing that they cannot complete the technique today, the teacher gives up and lets the students go to recess. This teacher had grand plans but tried to implement too much at once. Each step of this technique takes time to teach and time for students to get used to. Try one small step at a time when you are implementing a new technique.

Secondary Example of Group Reflecting on Learning

This example can be any secondary class at the end of any lesson.

The students are finishing up their work and turning it in. The teacher pulls out a stack of reflection questions printed and cut to size. There are two reflection questions:

"What did you do well in class today?" and "How did you contribute to someone else's learning today?" The students have seen the cards before, so they know what to expect. As they turn in their work, each student picks up a card with one of the questions on it without reading it first. They return to their desks and quietly write their names, the date, and their response to the question. As more students turn in their work, students with the same question start to find each other. When both are done writing, they discuss their answers to their question. All of this is done without whole-class direction. The teacher helps facilitate some of the match ups and ensures that all students are writing their responses before discussing. There is no need to explain the directions because the teacher established this routine long ago. Students spend the last few minutes of class discussing their responses and commenting on each other's answers. The teacher can hear compliments and advice throughout the room. As the students talk, the mood in the atmosphere becomes more jovial as they discuss their actions in class today and celebrate each other's participation. The teacher walks around listening, joining in the celebrations and conversations.

When the bell rings, students leave their responses in the basket by the door. The teacher then seeks out the responses of the students he has not already read to see how they reflected on their learning that day.

Secondary Nonexample of Group Reflecting on Learning

This teacher has not tried this technique before but wants to help students by letting them hear the responses of all the students in the class. With that in mind, he has students write their responses to the questions, and then asks them to share their answers with the class as a whole. This takes a long time, and students quit listening after the first few responses.

It is seldom an effective use of class time for every student to respond to a question one at a time.

Determining If Students Can Reflect on Learning in Groups

The only way to know if students can effectively reflect on their learning in groups is for you to witness them doing it. Plan in advance how you will monitor so that you are prepared and have time allotted for this crucial step. Here are some monitoring techniques you might use:

- Listen as students explain why their partners rated themselves where they did on the scale.

- Students think of one word to describe what they did well on their work. Ask students to tell you their partner's word.

- Students list two things on a sticky note they will do to improve their status as a result of their conversations and put them on the class door on the way out.

- Students write examples of how their partners demonstrated the learning target on a whiteboard. As you walk around listening to conversations, read over the examples.

The student proficiency scale for group reflecting on learning found in Table 7.1 will help you assess whether your students are on their way to or are already exhibiting the desired result of this technique.

Table 7.1: Student Proficiency Scale for Group Reflecting on Learning

Emerging	Fundamental	Desired Result
Students answer the reflection question.	Students explain their thinking about their own learning.	Students actively participate in a discussion about their progress in learning by explaining their learning and actively listening and interacting to their partner's response.
Students listen to their partner's response.	Students listen and respond to their partner's response.	Students can explain how the group interaction helped them identify next steps for growth.
Students accurately reflect on their learning.	Students identify next steps for growth.	

Scaffold and Extend Instruction to Meet Students' Needs

The way you scaffold or extend this particular technique depends on the reflection questions and the type of interaction you choose to implement in your class. Keep in mind specific students who may need these adaptations as you plan.

Scaffolding

- Provide a menu of questions for students who struggle with answering reflection questions.

- Provide sample answers and ask students to expand on them.

- Give students individual timers so they can set their own time limits.

- Provide a list of words, potentially vocabulary words from the critical content or words related to learning, that might help students discuss their own thinking about their learning.

- Tell students where you think they are on the proficiency scale and then have them explain to their partners why.

Extending

If student groups readily reflect on their learning, ask them to extrapolate to their life outside of school using the following suggestions:

- Ask students how what they did to contribute to their group today could be useful with their siblings.

- Ask students to compare each other's answers and make generalizations about learning in the unit.

- Ask students to brainstorm how they could help each other learn.

Conclusion

The goal of this guide is to enable teachers to become more effective in teaching content to their students. The beginning step, as you have learned in the preceding pages, is to become skilled at helping your students gain skills interacting with each other to learn content.

To determine if this goal has been met, you will need to gather information from your students, as well as solicit feedback from your supervisor or colleagues, to find someone willing to embark on this learning journey with you. Engage in meaningful self-reflection on your use of the strategy. If you acquire nothing else from this guide, let it be the importance of *monitoring*. The tipping point in your level of expertise and your students' achievement is *monitoring*. Implementing this strategy well is not enough. Your goal is the desired result: evidence that your students have developed a deeper understanding of the content.

To be most effective, view implementation as a three-step process:

- Implement the strategy using your energy and creativity to adopt and adapt the various techniques in this guide. Organize your students to learn content by interacting with each other and sharing perspectives.

- Monitor for the desired result. In other words, while you are implementing the technique, determine whether that technique is effective with the students. For organizing students to learn, check to see if your students show better understanding of the content because they have interacted with each other.

- If, as a result of your monitoring, you realize that your instruction was not adequate for students to achieve the desired result, seek out ways to change or adapt your approach by either scaffolding or extending so that *all* students show gains from interacting with each other and sharing perspectives.

Although you can certainly experience this guide and gain expertise independently, the process will be more beneficial if you read and work through its contents with colleagues.

Reflection and Discussion Questions

Use the following reflection and discussion questions during a team meeting or even as food for thought prior to a meeting with your coach, mentor, or supervisor:

1. How has your instruction changed as a result of reading and implementing the instructional techniques found in this book?

2. What ways have you found to modify and enhance the instructional techniques found in this book to scaffold and extend your instruction?

3. What was your biggest challenge, in terms of implementing this instructional strategy?

4. How would you describe the changes in your students' learning that have occurred as a result of implementing this instructional strategy?

5. What will you do to share what you have learned with colleagues at your grade level or in your department?

The best way to increase instructional expertise is to implement, monitor, and analyze your students' learning growth. Years of research science has shown that this strategy, *organizing for learning,* will increase student achievement and learning, but *only* when implemented with artful teaching judgment and experience displayed by good teachers. It is this masterful combination of the art and the science of teaching that creates the richest learning environments, the most satisfaction for teachers, and the best results for students.

References

Arizona Department of Education. (2006). *The Arizona Standards for Visual Arts*. Retrieved March 31, 2015, from https://www.azed.gov/standards-practices /files/2011/09/visualarts.pdf

Common Core State Standards Initiative. (2010). *Common Core State Standards for Mathematics*. Retrieved March 31, 2015 from http://www.corestandards.org/ wp-content/uploads/Math_Standards.pdf

Commonwealth of Massachusetts Department of Education. (2003). *Massachusetts History and Social Science Framework*. Retrieved March 31, 2015, from http://www.doe.mass.edu/frameworks/hss/final.pdf

de Bono, E. (1999). *Six thinking hats*. New York: Little, Brown and Company.

Dickson, S. V., Collins, V. L., Simmons, D. C., & Kame'enui, E. J. (1998). Metacognitive strategies: Instructional and curricular basics and implications. In D. C. Simmons & E. J. Kame'enui (Eds.), *What reading research tells us about children with diverse learning needs* (pp. 361–380). Hillsdale, NJ: Erlbaum.

Fisher, D., & Frey, N. (2007). *Checking for understanding: Formative assessment techniques for your classroom*. Alexandria, VA: Association for Supervision and Curriculum Development.

Fisher, D., & Frey, N. (2014). *Better learning through structured teaching: A framework for the gradual release of responsibility*. Alexandria, VA: Association for Supervision and Curriculum Development.

Frey, N., Fisher, D., & Everlove, S. (2009). *Productive group work: How to engage students, build teamwork, and promote understanding*. Alexandria, VA: Association for Supervision and Curriculum Development.

Hattie, J. (2008). *Visible learning: A synthesis of over 800 meta-analyses relating to achievement*. New York: Routledge.

Johnson, D. W. (1975). *Learning together and alone: Cooperation, competition, and individualization*. New York: Prentice Hall.

Johnson, D. W., & Johnson, R. T. (2005). *Teaching students to be peacemakers*. Minneapolis, MN: Burgess Publishing Company.

Johnson, D. W., Johnson, R. W., & Stanne, M. B. (2000). *Cooperative learning methods: A meta-analysis*. Retrieved March 31, 2015, from http://www.tablelearning.com/uploads/File/EXHIBIT-B.pdf

Johnson, D. W., & Roger, T. (2003). *Assessing students in groups: Promoting group responsibility and individual accountability.* Thousand Oaks, CA: Corwin.

Kagan, S. (2009). *Cooperative learning.* San Clemente, CA: Kagan Cooperative Learning.

Marzano, R. J. (1992). *A different kind of learning: Teaching with dimensions of learning.* Alexandria, VA: Association of Supervision and Curriculum Development.

Marzano, R. J. (2007). *The art and science of teaching: A comprehensive framework for effective instruction.* Alexandria, VA: Association for Supervision and Curriculum Development.

Marzano, R. J. (with T. Boogren, T. Heflebower, J. Kanold-McIntyre, & D. Pickering). (2012). *Becoming a reflective teacher.* Bloomington, IN: Marzano Research Laboratory.

Marzano, R. J., & Brown, J. L. (2009). *Handbook for the art and science of teaching.* Alexandria, VA: Association for Supervision and Curriculum Development.

Marzano, R. J., Carbaugh, B., Rutherford, A., & Toth, M. D. (2014). *Marzano Center teacher observation protocol for the 2014 Marzano Teacher Evaluation Model.* West Palm Beach, FL: Learning Sciences International.

Marzano, R. J., & Heflebower, T. (2012). *Teaching and assessing 21st century skills.* Bloomington, IN: Solution Tree Press.

Marzano, R. J., & Simms, J. A. (with T. Roy, T. Heflebower, & P. Warrick). (2013). *Coaching classroom instruction.* Bloomington, IN: Marzano Research Laboratory.

Marzano, R. J., & Toth, M. D. (2013). *Deliberate practice for deliberate growth: Teacher evaluation systems for continuous instructional improvement.* West Palm Beach, FL: Learning Sciences International.

Marzano, R. J., Yanoski, D. C., Hoegh, J. K., & Simms, J. A. (2013). *Using Common Core Standards to enhance classroom instruction and assessment.* Bloomington, IN: Marzano Research Laboratory.

National Council for the Social Studies (NCSS). (2013). *The College, Career, and Civic Life (C3) Frame for Social Studies State Standards: Guidance for enhancing the rigor or K–12 Civics, Economics, Geography, and History.* Silver Spring, MD: NCSS.

Next Generation Science Standards: For states, by states. (2013). Retrieved March 31, 2015, from http://www.nextgenscience.org/next-generation-science-standards

Perini, M. J., & Silver, H. F. (2012). *The core six: Essential strategies for achieving excellence with the Common Core.* Boston, MA: Heinle ELT.

Index

A

active processing. *See* grouping for active processing

C

CCR (College and Career Readiness) Anchor Standards
    defined, 2
    for Speaking and Listening, 25
CCSS (Common Core State Standards), 3
    defined, 2
collaborative learning, 6
compass partners form, 89, 90
conative skills
    See also name of instructional technique
    defined, 6–7
conflicts, handling, 65–67
content
    See also critical content, identifying
    defined, 2
cooperative learning, 6
cooperative projects
    common mistakes, avoiding, 67
    conative skills, teaching and reinforcing, 65–67
    critical content, identifying, 61–62
    description of technique, 61
    difference between structured grouping and, 61
    examples and nonexamples, 68–70
    grouping students, methods for, 64–65
    implementation, 61–67

    interactions, structuring student, 63–64
    monitoring for desired result, 70–71
    routines, establishing, 65
    scaffolding and extending instruction, 72
    student proficiency scale, 71
    tasks, planning meaningful, 62–63
critical content, identifying, 8
    See also name of instructional technique

D

declarative knowledge, 5
desired result
    See also name of instructional technique
    defined, 2
    monitoring, 9–10

E

extending, defined, 2
extending instruction
    See also name of instructional technique
    meeting students' needs and, 10–11

F

feedback. *See* peer response group

G

graphic organizers, use of, 87–88

Notes

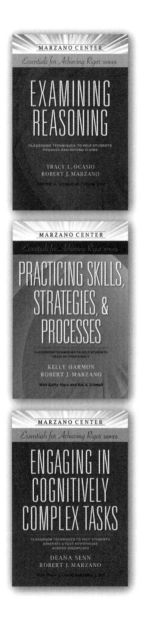